Home Office Research Study 235

Mobile phone theft

Victoria Harrington and Pat Mayhew

The views expressed in this report are those of the authors, not necessarily those of the Home Office (nor do they reflect Government policy).

Home Office Research, Development and Statistics Directorate
December 2001

Home Office Research Studies

The Home Office Research Studies are reports on research undertaken by or on behalf of the Home Office. They cover the range of subjects for which the Home Secretary has responsibility. Other publications produced by the Research, Development and Statistics Directorate include Findings, Statistical Bulletins and Statistical Papers.

The Research, Development and Statistics Directorate

RDS is part of the Home Office. The Home Office's purpose is to build a safe, just and tolerant society in which the rights and responsibilities of individuals, families and communities are properly balanced and the protection and security of the public are maintained.

RDS is also part of National Statistics (NS). One of the aims of NS is to inform Parliament and the citizen about the state of the nation and provide a window on the work and performance of government, allowing the impact of government policies and actions to be assessed.

Therefore -

Research Development and Statistics Directorate exists to improve policy making, decision taking and practice in support of the Home Office purpose and aims, to provide the public and Parliament with information necessary for informed debate and to publish information for future use.

First published 2001

Application for reproduction should be made to the Communication Development Unit, Room 201, Home Office, 50 Queen Anne's Gate, London SW1H 9AT.

Acknowledgements

We would like to thank those police forces that kindly provided data for analysis in this study. In particular our thanks go to the four Basic Command Units (Westminster, Birmingham, Bristol and Stockport) that allowed time and space for a number of researchers from RDS to collect and record information from robbery case files.

Several researchers in the Crime and Criminal Justice Unit of RDS assisted in the collection of data for this report. However, special thanks must go to Geoff Newiss and Jonathan Smith from the Police and Reducing Crime Unit of the Home Office. Jonathan's help and advice in finalising the data set and in the latter stages of the study were invaluable.

Finally, thanks must go to Feltham Young Offenders' Institute for allowing us to interview a number of young people and to the young people themselves for speaking so frankly about this type of crime.

Victoria Harrington
Pat Mayhew

Foreword

There is currently a dearth of research concerning mobile phone theft. However, the marked increase in mobile phone ownership in the last few years, particularly among young people, has made mobile phones an attractive target for theft. The fact that, among young users in particular, mobile phones are frequently on display only adds to their vulnerability.

The report concentrates heavily upon robberies in which mobile phones are involved. Concern over the recent rise in robbery offences and claims that the rise was fuelled by phone robberies, led the Home Office to set up several Working Groups. This research was undertaken to service the Publicity Working Group.

The report draws on a number of sources of information. Initially it focuses upon all mobile phone theft and estimates both levels and trends in recent years. Using a number of self-report surveys the risk of having a phone stolen for both adults and young people over the age of ten is estimated.

Mobile phone robberies are the main focus in the remainder of the study and consideration is given to the question of how far the recent increase in robbery has been fuelled by mobile phone thefts. From both data provided by police forces and the examination of case files from four central city Basic Command Units the characteristics of those accused and suspects of this type of robbery are examined. Similarly, the characteristics of victims of mobile phone robbery are scrutinised, as are some of the circumstances of this type of robbery in central city areas.

DAVID MOXON
Crime and Criminal Justice Unit

Contents

		Page
Acknowledgements		i
Foreword		ii
Summary		ix
1.	**Introduction**	**1**
	Plan of the report	3
2.	**The extent of phone theft: current evidence**	**5**
	British Crime Survey estimate	5
	The 'On Track' survey estimate	7
	The MORI survey	8
	Estimates from six police forces	9
3.	**Features of phone thefts**	**13**
	Which crimes generate the most thefts?	13
	Which offences involve phones most	
	in proportionate terms	15
	Robbery	17
	The concentration of phone robberies in city centres	17
	Phone-only robberies and those in	
	which other items are taken	18
4.	**Trends in phone thefts overall**	**21**
	The British Crime Survey	21
	Police figures	21

5.	**Trends in phone robbery**	**25**
	Changes in the proportion of robberies involving phones	25
	The change in phone robberies relative to other offences	26
	Personal and commercial robberies	28
	The growth in phone robberies involving only a phone	28
	The effect of phone robbery on the increase in robbery offences	29
	The effect on the longer-term trend in robbery	31
6.	**Offenders in phone robberies**	**35**
	Gender of offenders	35
	Age of offenders	37
	Ethnicity	40
	Lone or multiple suspects	42
7	**Victims of phone robbery**	**45**
	Gender of victims	45
	The gender victim /suspect interaction	46
	Age of victims	47
	Ethnicity of victims	50
	Whether the phone was in use or on display	51
	The time of offences	52
	The day of the week	53
8	**Conclusions**	**55**
	Some technical points	57
	Why phones are stolen	58
	The uses to which stolen phones are put	58
	Prevention: some issues	59
	Prevention: the present results	61
References		**65**
Appendix A: Additional tables		**67**

Figures and tables

Figure 1.1   UK mobile phone subscribers   1

Table 2.1   Risks of phone theft for adults 1999/2000,
by offence types: British Crime Survey   7

Figure 2.1   Risks of phone thefts per 100,000 population
in six police forces   9

Figure 3.1   Offences in which mobile phones are most often
targeted against adults (2001 and 2000 BCS)   13

Table 3.1   Offences in which mobile phones were
most often targeted in 2000/01 (four police forces)   14

Figure 3.2   Proportion of each offence type involving
a phone theft: 2000 BCS   15

Figure 3.3   Proportion of each offence type involving
a phone theft in 2000/01: the MPD and three other forces   16

Figure 3.4   Risks of phone robbery per 100,000
population in six forces   17

Figure 3.5   Percentage of robberies involving phones in
BCUs and forces, 2000-01   18

Table 3.2   Phone robberies at BCU level: personal
and commercial robbery   19

Table 4.1   British Crime Survey estimates of mobile
phone thefts (those aged 16 or more)   21

Figure 4.1   Percentage increase in thefts involving
phones in six police forces   22

Table 4.2   Growth of all recorded offences involving phones, six forces   23

Figure 5.1   The proportion of robberies involving phones
over the last three years   26

Figure 5.2   Percentage change in mobile phone thefts
for each offence type: 1998/99-2000/01   27

Figure 5.3   Numbers of personal and business robberies
1998/00 to 2000/01   28

Figure 5.4	Percentage change in personal robberies for phone-only incidents and those in which phones were taken with other items	29
Figure 5.5	Trends in robbery and theft and handling offences recorded by the police since 1990	30
Table 5.1	Robbery and phone robbery trends between 1998/999 and 2000/01	31
Figure 5.6	Trends in robberies and theft and handling offences recorded by the police since 1990, with adjustment for phone robberies.	32
Figure 5.7	Trends in robberies recorded by the police since 1990, with adjustment for phone-only robberies.	33
Table 6.1	Gender of those involved in phone robberies	36
Figure 6.1	The age of offenders for the combined forces of MPD, West Midlands and Avon and Somerset	37
Table 6.2	Age of accused: percentage of all those accused (police force information)	38
Figure 6.2	Age of phone robbery and non-phone robbery suspects: BCU information	39
Table 6.3	Ethnic breakdown of force populations	40
Figure 6.3	Those accused of phone robbery, by ethnicity (police force information)	41
Figure 6.4	Those suspected of phone robbery, by ethnicity (BCU information)	41
Figure 6.5	Lone and multiple suspects (BCU information)	43
Figure 6.6	Multiple suspects in phone and non-phone robberies (BCU information)	43
Figure 6.7	Lone and group offending, by ethnicity (BCU information)	44
Table 7.1	The gender of victims in phone robberies	45
Table 7.2	Offenders and victims: % of all incidents (BCU information)	46
Table 7.3	Gender differences in suspects and victims (BCU information)	47
Figure 7.1	Age of victims as a percentage of all victims (combined force and BCU results)	47
Figure 7.2	Percentage of victims under 18: phone and non-phone robbery (BCU information	48
Figure 7.3	The age profile of victims and suspects (BCU information)	49
Figure 7.4	Age of victims by gender (MPD, West Midlands and Avon and Somerset average)	49

Figure 7.5	Ethnicity of victims, by police force	50
Table 7.4	Ethnicity of victims in each BCU	51
Figure 7.6	Time of occurrence: phone and non-phone robberies (BCU information)	52
Figure 7.7	Time of occurrence: phone robberies by age (BCU information)	53
Figure 7.8	The day on which phone and non-phone robberies occur (BCU information)	53
Table A2.1	Proportion of each offence type involving a phone theft in 2000/01: four police forces	67
Table A4.1	Percentage change in thefts involving phones in six forces	67
Table A4.2	The proportion of thefts from the person involving phones over the last three years, six forces	68
Table A5.1	Robbery and phone robbery trends	69
Table A5.2	Personal robberies for phone-only incidents and those in which phones were taken with other items	70
Table A6.1	Age of accused: percentage of all those accused (police force information)	70
Table A6.2	Age of suspects: percentage of all suspects (BCU information)	71
Table A6.3	Ethnicity of suspects (BCU information)	72
Table A6.4	Number of suspects for each offence	72
Table A6.5	Lone and multiple offenders (BCU information)	73
Table A7.1	Breakdown of victims and offenders (percentages): phone and non-phone robberies (BCU information)	73
Table A7.2	Age of victims, by gender (police force information)	74
Table A7.3	Age of victims (BCU information)	74
Table A7.4	Age and types of robbery (BCU information)	75

In the scale of things, mobile phones are relatively new, and awareness of the problem of phone theft newer still. It is unsurprising therefore that there has been little research to date. This report presents findings on thefts of mobile phones ('phone thefts'). These emanate from a number of different offences of which robbery is one, but there is particular focus on robberies involving mobile phones ('phone robberies'). Different sources of information are drawn upon:

- The British Crime Survey (BCS) for estimates of levels and trends in phone thefts.

- Information from up to seven police forces on phone thefts, and trends over time.

- Two recent schools surveys in which pupils were asked whether they had a phone stolen in the last year.

- Information from three police forces on those accused of phone robberies.

- Analysis of police robbery records in four central city Basic Command Units (BCUs), providing details of suspects and victims of phone robberies.

- Interviews with offenders in Feltham Young Offenders' Institution who had been involved in phone robbery.

The extent of phone theft

- The number of phones currently being stolen is unknown. There are no consolidated figures from either phone operators or insurers. Police figures will not cover unreported offences, but may include a much small number of false allegations of theft. Existing surveys provide figures with inevitable sampling error, and no coverage of commercial targets.

The BCS estimate

- The BCS provides an estimate of phone thefts against those aged 16 or more. It suggests there were about 470,000 phone thefts (including attempts) in 2000 originating from a number of different offences, robbery one of them. This figure is based on 1 per cent of people having a phone stolen once or more – or an estimated 2 per cent of phone owners.

- The BCS results indicate that adults are as likely to fall victim when a phone is left in a car, when their house is broken into, or when they leave the phone unattended somewhere else (e.g., the office or a restaurant). The chances of phones being stolen in either a robbery or a theft from the person are no higher. Thefts from the person are akin to robbery: they involve stealth theft without any direct force or threat of force, in which case robbery would apply.

The school survey estimates

- The much larger of the two school surveys (the 'On Track' survey) asked 15,000 11–15 year olds whether they had a phone stolen in the last year. Grossed up risk figures suggest there were 550,000 phone thefts against this age group between mid-2000 and mid-2001: 12% said they had been victimised at least once. There is reason, though, to be cautious of the figures mainly because the surveys were conducted in deprived areas.

- The smaller MORI survey of 5,000 11–16 years olds early in 2001 suggested at least 200,000 phone thefts against the age group in the last year. Five per cent said they had a phone stolen at least once – less than half the level in the On Track survey, but well in excess of the 1 per cent for adults.

- The On Track survey indicates that the difference in risks for teenagers and adults of having a phone stolen in a robbery or theft from the person is particularly wide.

Offences recorded by the police

- On the basis of figures from six police forces extrapolated to England and Wales, there were an estimated 330,000 offences involving phones recorded by the police (Table A). These are both phones stolen as well as attempts to steal a phone. This will underestimate the total, as not all thefts will be reported. Some reports may be false allegations – although they were not judged large.

Table A   Best estimates

	Coverage		Limitations		Strengths	Latest period	Coverage	Best estimate All phone thefts
British Crime Survey	E&W, those aged 16 or more	Sampling error	Adults (age 16+) only	No coverage of commercial targets	Covers unreported offences	2000	Thefts and attempts	470,000
On Track schools survey	E&W, 11-15 year olds. N = 15,000	Sampling error	Deprived areas	Exaggeration?	Covers unreported offences	Mid 2000-2001	Thefts only	550,000
MORI schools survey	E&W, 11-16 year olds. N = 5,000	Sampling error	Small sample		Covers unreported offences	Early 2000 to early 2001	Thefts only	200,000
Best estimate from surveys	11 years upwards	Sampling error		No coverage of commercial targets	Includes unreported offences			**710,000**
Offences recorded by the police	E & W	Reported offences only	False allegations	Based on sample of forces	What the police deal with	2000/01	Thefts and attempts	330,000

Note: Half the weight is given to the On Track schools survey to that of the MORI schools survey

Features of phone thefts

- All told, 5.5 per cent of all incidents counted by the BCS involved the theft (or attempted theft) of a phone in 2000 – albeit often along with other property. Police figures show a similar 6 per cent of all recorded crimes in 2000/01. The proportion was higher in metropolitan forces.

In quantitative terms

- In quantitative terms, more phones are targeted in offences *other than robbery* according to both police figures and the BCS.

The BCS

- The BCS indicates a third of phone thefts in 2000 came from miscellaneous thefts, and nearly as many from thefts from vehicles. Phones stolen in robberies and thefts from the person made up about 20% of all offences.

Police figures

- The police figures showed that four in ten phones were stolen in 'other' types of theft and about two in ten from cars. Differences in the proportions from the BCS are not unexpected, given different coverage and the extent to which some offences are reported more than others.

- About 20% of recorded offences involving phones were in the course of personal robberies or thefts from the person – the same as the BCS.

In proportionate terms
The BCS

- The BCS indicates that thefts from the person, miscellaneous thefts and burglary most often involved a phone (about one in ten did). The figures for some other offences, including robbery, were not much different.

Police figures

- Police figures show a much higher proportion of phones stolen in robberies and thefts from the person than the BCS. (In the MPD, for instance, a full 36% of robberies involved phones and the average figure for thefts from the person was a third.) These higher figures may be because the BCS excludes young victims, and reporting differences across each offence. False allegations may also be an issue.

- The results suggest robbery in city centre areas is more likely to involve phones than in police forces as a whole (Figure A). This may be because the types of offenders in the business of stealing phones (even if along with other things) may frequent city centres themselves more. Or busy central areas may provide the easiest pickings from other young socialites or busy shoppers.

Figure A   % of robberies involving phones in BCUs and forces

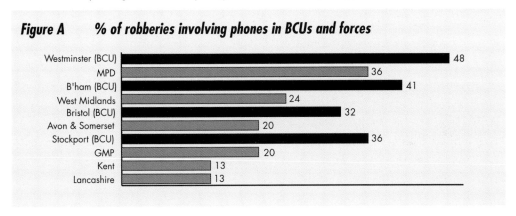

Trends in all phone thefts

The results show a substantial growth in offences involving the theft of phones. A key issue, though, is whether this is because phones are being specifically targeted. It could, of course, be that phones are just 'stealable' items, and their increasing appearance in thefts reflects greater ownership.

The BCS

- The BCS indicates that 16% more phones were stolen in 2000 than in 1999, and 190% more than in 1995. The increase in thefts is less since 1995 than the increase in phone subscribers (which was up virtually 600%).

Police figures

- Figures from six forces suggest that the number of recorded phone thefts has at least doubled within two years – i.e., between 1998/999 and 2000/01. There was a higher (three-fold) increase in the West Midlands and Lancashire.

- The police figures suggest the *rise* in incidents involving phones was greater between 1998/999 and 1999/00 than between 1999/00 and 2000/01. This applies to all phone thefts and phone robberies.

Robbery trends

The emphasis was on how far one can say that phones have fuelled the recent rise in robbery. A number of pointers were drawn from figures over the past three years:

- There was an increase in the proportion of robberies involving phones – from about 8% in 1998/99 (an estimated 5,500 phone robberies) to about 28% in 2000/01 (an estimated 26,300 phone robberies). (The picture is similar for thefts from the person.)

- Figures from four forces show the rise in phone *robberies* over the two years 1998/999 to 2000/01 was generally greater than for other offences involving phones (Figure B). The figures are extrapolated from four forces to England and Wales, and are therefore estimates.

Figure B   % change in crimes involving phones: 1998/99 to 2000/01

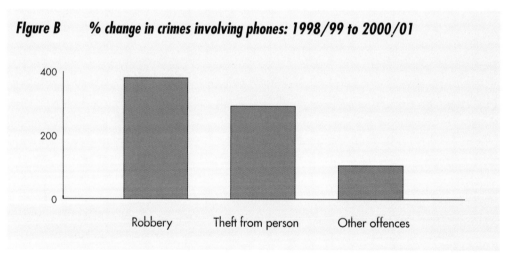

- Information from six forces shows the increase in *phone* robberies was much greater than for robbery as a whole. Part of the increase will be due simply to greater phone ownership. Some may also be due to more false allegations as a corollary of higher ownership. In addition some may be because there is more reporting to the police as phone ownership has grown in particular among youngsters for whom a phone will be a particularly valuable item.

- There was a higher increase in *phone* robberies that involve *only* a phone, as opposed to those that involved a phone and other items.

Also considered were robbery trends over the 1990s as a whole, and what the trend recently might have looked liked if phone robberies are taken out of the figures.

- Robbery trends have had a different dynamic from other crime (measured for technical reasons by theft and handling). Thefts peaked in 1993, since when they have fallen. Recorded robberies, in contrast, increased in most years. Whatever caused the increases in robberies in the early to mid-1990s, then, it was unlikely to be mobile phones since ownership levels were low. (The trend in thefts from the person has been generally similar to robbery, with an increase since 1990 rather higher than robbery.)

- The trend in robbery since 1990 can be re-drawn (Figure C) to account for the differential changes in phone and non-phone robberies. This involves estimation. Theft offences are a comparator. The trend line for 'robberies less all phone robberies' is much shallower, with a levelling off in the past two years. However, it would be unrealistic to see this as a true indicator of what the situation might have been. This is because some of the robberies excluded may have taken place anyway. The fact that a phone was stolen may simply reflect the fact that they are now prominent among the smaller, higher value 'stealable' items that people carry on them.

- A more stringent test of what the overall robbery trend might have been is to exclude incidents in which *only* a phone was taken. This is on the premise that phone-only incidents are more likely to be specifically due to phones than robberies where a phone was taken with other items. The recent trend in robberies excluding phone-only incidents is rather more favourable than all robberies (an 8% increase instead of 13%), but less so than robberies with *all* phone incidents excluded.

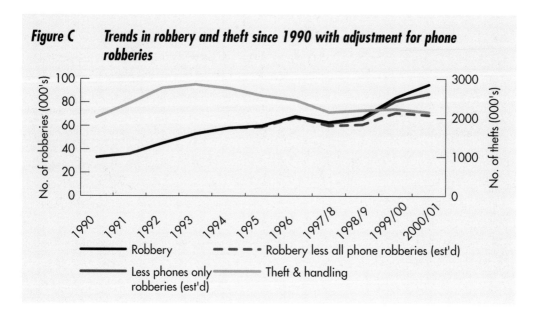

Figure C   Trends in robbery and theft since 1990 with adjustment for phone robberies

Legend:
——— Robbery   – – – · Robbery less all phone robberies (est'd)
——— Less phones only ———— Theft & handling
robberies (est'd)

Offenders

Information on those accused of phone robberies in 2000–01 was available from three forces. There were about 2,000 cases from the MPD, but fewer in Avon & Somerset and the West Midlands. There was also information from the four BCUs on those suspected (i.e., not necessarily accused) of phone and non-phone robbery in the first three months of 2001. There were about 200 cases in each BCU.

Gender

- The overwhelming majority of offenders were male – an average of about 90% in the forces and over 90% in the BCUs. There is a hint, then, that phone robbery in city centres is even more of a male pursuit than in other areas.

Age

- Many of those accused of phone robbery were young, but the proportions differed. Two-thirds were under 18 in the MPD, and more than this in the Stockport BCU. In contrast, only about half of those accused in the West Midlands and Avon & Somerset were under 18, and less than a third in Bristol. This illustrates the diversity of phone robbery in different areas.

- The peak age of offending was 16, although this was influenced by the dominance of the MPD's figures. A third of all offenders were aged 15 or 16.

- Those involved in phone robbery were younger than other robbers. (There was only BCU data on this.) Over half of phone robbery suspects were said to be under 18, but less than a third of others.

- According to both the accused and the suspect data, female offenders were rather younger than males. In the forces, for instance, about 80% of females accused were under 18, compared with about 60% of males.

Ethnicity
- Both the force and BCU data indicated that the overwhelming majority of phone robbers were black (see Figure D).

Figure D   *Those accused of phone robbery, by ethnicity*

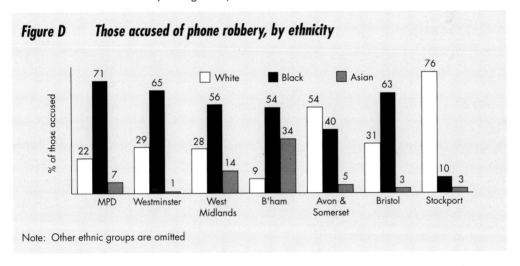

Note: Other ethnic groups are omitted

- Asians made up a third of suspects in Birmingham. This was well in excess of any other BCU and will partly reflect the higher Asian population in the West Midlands. Most offenders (76%) were white in Stockport.

Lone and multiple suspects
- More than two-thirds of incidents involved offenders working with others. This was a higher proportion than for non-phone robberies (BCU information).

- Slightly more female offenders worked with others than males. Younger offenders, too, more often operated in groups (80% of those under 18). Whites also more frequently did so than blacks, although Asians most often of all operated with others.

Victims

Up to seven police force areas provided information on victims in 2000/01, although not all forces provided the same details. Information on the victims of phone robberies in the first three months of 2000/01 was also available from the four BCUs. Again, some comparisons can be made between phone and non-phone robberies.

Gender

- About four out of five victims were male, although London had rather more female victims.

- With the preponderance of male offenders, phone robbery is very much a male-on-male activity – as of course is the case with most other non-domestic interpersonal crime. Of all incidents, 77% involved males-on-males (Table B). The figure was slightly lower (71%) for non-phone robberies.

Table B   Offenders and victims: % of all incidents (BCU information)

Male offenders(s): male victim	77%
Male offenders(s): female victim	14%
Female offender(s): female victim	4%
Mixed group offenders: female victim	2%
Mixed group offenders: male victim	2%
Female offender(s): male victim	1%
	100%

- Although most incidents against women were perpetrated by men, a third involved female offenders or mixed groups. These were very unusual when men were targeted.

Age

- Those under 18 constituted nearly half (48%) of all victims, with the peak at age 15 and 16. Those aged 18 to 29 constituted nearly 40% of victims. (These results are based on all the force and BCU information.)

- The picture varied somewhat by area. In Stockport a full 80% of victims were under 18 – mirroring the unusually young age of offenders there. In contrast, there were fewer than average younger victims in Lancashire and Bristol.

- In all BCUs except Bristol, victims of phone robbery were younger than victims of other types of robbery.

- In Stockport and Westminster, there was little difference in the age profile of victims who had only a phone taken, and those who had a phone stolen along with other things. In Bristol and Birmingham, though, victims of phone-only robberies were younger than others.

Age of victims and offenders

- In phone robberies, the age of victims was more evenly distributed than that of offenders. The effect of this is that there were both more younger victims than younger suspects, and more older victims than older suspects. This suggests that many offenders prey on victims both younger and older than themselves. Figure E shows details from the BCUs.

Figure E   ***Age profile of victims and suspects: % all each group***

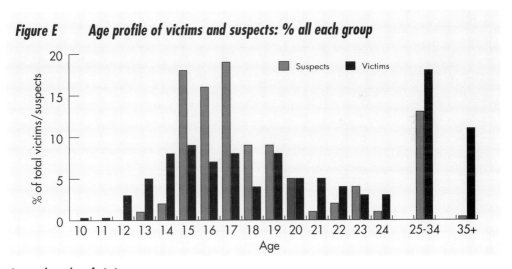

Age and gender of victims

- Female victims were older than male victims. In the three forces about 70% of females were 18 and over, as against 50% of males. The figures from the BCUs were very similar. Female victims of other robberies were also older.

- Figures from the GMP show that the proportion of younger victims (under 19) has increased from 35% in 1998/99 to 46% in 2000/01. It might be that younger children feature more in phone robberies simply as a consequence of the greater likelihood of them owning a phone, and the fact that they are probably especially likely to report the loss of a phone to the police (as it will be an important item to them).

Ethnicity of victims

- The vast majority of victims in phone robberies were whites. Asians were next most often targeted. This was particularly so in the West Midlands (where they constituted nearly a quarter of victims) and in the MPD.

Whether the phone was in use or on display

- In 23% of incidents overall victims were using their phone or had it on display when it was targeted. The figure in Westminster was higher.

The time of offences

- The picture was similar for phone and non-phone robberies although very slightly more phone robberies took place in the afternoon. This information related to January to March 2001. Lighter and warmer evenings in other parts of the year might increase the proportion of evening and night robberies.

- The indications are that phone robberies in the early hours mainly involved victims over 18. In contrast, nearly six in ten phone robberies against those under 18 took place between 2pm and 10pm. Different activity patterns will underlie the difference to an extent.

Section 8 discusses the preventive implications of these results.

1.   Introduction

Mobile phones have become a staple of modern day living for many in the UK. The first phones were marketed in about 1985, but were large and relatively expensive. The market changed substantially in the 1990s to smaller, cheaper phones mainly taken out on contract initially. Pay-As-You-Go phones opened up ownership to those who did not wish or were not able to take out a contract. Oftel figures show a substantial growth in ownership, with the increase particularly marked in the last two years (Figure 1.1). The latest (2001) survey indicates that 70% of UK adults own or use a mobile phone. Ownership among young people is even higher.[1] The dominance of pre-pay phones is now clear: a MORI survey for Oftel in May 2001 showed that four out of five users had them, and 90% of new phone sales in the last 12 months were pre-pay.

Figure 1.1   UK mobile phone subscribers

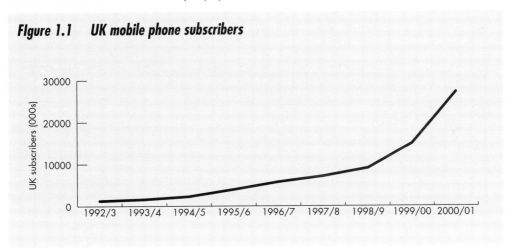

As a small, potentially valuable item, high on 'image' for the young in particular, it was probably inevitable that mobile phones would become an attractive target for theft. The fact that they are frequently on display adds to their vulnerability. So too does their undeniable technological wizardry – *pace* the way in which they are ostentatiously used and 'played with'. One offender talked to in the course of this research was eloquent in describing the 'magic' of being able to talk to anyone anywhere "without wires". Indeed, after denigrating the idea that the problem of phone theft was anything other than a matter of increasing availability, his eulogy about mobile phone technology perhaps gave his game away.

---

1   In a survey at the end of 2000, 81% of 15-24 year olds claimed they had a mobile phone, and in mid-2001 surveys discussed in this report, about the same proportion of 11-15 year olds said they were phone users.

This report presents results of research on the theft of mobile phones. These are called 'phone thefts' hereon for simplicity. Since some incidents involve only an attempted theft, the term 'targeted' is used to cover phones actually stolen as well as those where an attempt was made to do so. The report concentrates in particular on robberies in which mobile phones are involved ('phone robberies'). It draws on a number of sources of information:

- The British Crime Survey (BCS) for estimates of levels and trends in phone thefts, as well as the risks for adults of having a phone stolen.

- Provisional figures from a recent school survey of 15,000 11–15 year olds who were asked whether they had a phone stolen in the last year.

- A MORI survey early in 2001 of just over 5,000 school children aged 11–16 covering much the same ground.

- Information from up to six police forces on phone thefts in relation to all recorded crime, and trends over time.

- Information from three police forces on those accused of phone robberies.

- Analysis of police robbery records in four central city Basic Command Units (BCUs), providing details of suspects and victims of phone robberies.

- Interviews with eight offenders in Feltham Young Offenders' Institution, all of whom had been involved in phone robbery.

The background to this research was concern about the recent rise in robbery offences, which was evident both from the British Crime Survey (BCS) and offences recorded by the police. Claims were made – mainly on the basis of early evidence from the Metropolitan Police District (MPD) – that the rise in robbery was being fuelled by phone robberies, in particular incidents in which young offenders were targeting young victims. This led the Home Office to set up three Working Groups: a technical group, one on police and industry co-operation, and a third on publicity. The research reported here was undertaken by the Research, Statistics and Development Directorate of the Home Office to service the Publicity Working Group.

Notwithstanding the early MPD information, there was in fact little good evidence prior to this research on the extent of phone theft here or elsewhere (cf. Grabosky and Smith,

1998). The Parliamentary Office of Science and Technology estimated in 1995 that something like 175,000 mobile phones were being stolen a year – though the basis of the estimate was not given.

The lack of firm estimates is not altogether surprising:

- Phone operators in the UK will only know about stolen phones if the owner informs them to block the line. This will apply to owners on contract, but those on Pay-As-You-Go might only inform operators if an insurance claim is to be made.

- The plethora of insurance companies offering cover for mobile phone theft means that no consolidated insurance figures are available.

- Police figures only capture incidents reported to them and in any case by no means all forces have information on the number of offences specifically involving phones.

Plan of the report

The plan of this report is as follows:

- Section 2 provides some estimates of the number of phones stolen. It draws here on the BCS, the two schools surveys, and on police force data. This section also assesses how the number of phone thefts translates into annual risks for adults and teenagers.

- Section 3 deals with which types of offences generate most mobile phone thefts – bearing in mind that while much recent attention has been on robbery, phone thefts feature in a number of other offences. It also looks at some features of robberies that involve phones.

- Section 4 looks at trends in all phone thefts, both in terms of BCS results, and those from six police forces.

- Section 5 takes up trends in phone robberies in more detail, examining the question of how far the recent increase in robbery has been fuelled by phone thefts.

- Section 6 deals with information from three police forces on the characteristics of those accused of phone theft. It also looks at information from the four BCUs on suspects in phone robberies (i.e., not necessarily those accused of an offence).

- Section 7 looks at police force and BCU information on the characteristics of victims. It also examines some of the circumstances of robberies in the central city areas.

- Section 8 says something about the technicalities of using phones after they are stolen, and about motivation – drawing in part upon the interesting if small number of interviews with offenders. The main lessons of the research for prevention are also taken up.

2.   The extent of phone theft: current evidence

The work here provides various pointers to the number of mobile phones currently being stolen and targeted for theft. It cannot give a definitive figure. No single source captures the entire picture, and there is overlap between them. Discussed below are various estimates from:

i.   The **BCS** in relation to risks for adults.

ii. The **On Track survey** covering young people. This was large in size, but with a somewhat unrepresentative sample.

iii. The smaller **MORI survey** which had a more representative sample.

iv. **Offences recorded by the police** – extrapolated from the six forces that provided data.

Estimates of the *number* of phone incidents from the first three sources come from grossing up from survey risk estimates. Because risk estimates are from samples, there is sampling error attached to them. This also means that the estimated numbers of offences from survey sources are not precise. Estimates from police recorded crime figures are also based on a sample of forces, so that there is imprecision here too as regards overall estimates.

British Crime Survey estimate

The British Crime Survey (BCS) covers a large representative sample of people aged 16 or more in England and Wales (see Kershaw *et al.*, 2001).[2] The survey counts crimes in the year before fieldwork – 2000 in the case of the latest 2001 BCS. It covers crimes against households (e.g., burglary and thefts from vehicles), as well as personal crimes (e.g., thefts of personal property and robbery). The BCS covers incidents whether or not reported to the police.

---

2   Sample sizes have varied somewhat. The 2000 BCS had a sample of about 20,000. The 2001 BCS – the first of a now annual (rather than biennial) series was larger in scale (40,000). However, the move to annual surveys involved some changes in design. Of the 2001 sample, a sub-sample were interviewed under 'old' design procedures, to maintain full comparability. The 2001 BCS results reported in this report are based on these 9,000 respondents.

The BCS suggests that there were 1.1 incidents per 100 people in 2000 in which a mobile phone was targeted in some crime measured by the survey. (Roughly 10% were attempts). As many respondents would not have had a phone, the figure for owners might be in the region of 2.1 incidents per 100 owners.[3]

The 1.1 per 100 figure is an 'incidence' measure, which takes into account the fact that some people will have experienced more than one theft. Another common measure of vulnerability is a 'prevalence risk': the proportion of those who had a phone stolen *once or more* in the year. For 2000, the BCS prevalence risk was 1.0 per cent – or 2 per cent for owners.

Grossing up from the incidence risk, the best BCS estimate is that **there were about 470,000 mobile phones stolen in incidents involving householders in 2000**.[4] This will underestimate the full number of phones targeted, since the BCS does not cover incidents against commercial targets, and it excludes those under 16.

BCS figures are somewhat fragile to estimate risks of phone theft in particular types of offences but with this caveat, Table 2.1 presents results from the 2000 and 2001 BCS, expressed per 100 adults.

Phones are most likely to be stolen in thefts from vehicles, then thefts of personal property (e.g. attended phones stolen from offices, restaurants etc). The chance of phones being stolen in robberies and theft from the person *together* (0.23 incidents per 100 people) is not too dissimilar. Theft from the person is akin to robbery; it involves stealth theft without any direct force or threat of force, in which case robbery would apply. (Pickpocketing from a bag would count as theft from the person.)

---

3   This uses an estimated 52% ownership figure for those aged 16 or more in 2000 (OFTEL figures provide the guide). The offences (attempts included) taken for BCS analysis were: robbery, thefts from the person, thefts of personal property, burglary, thefts of and from vehicles, and other household thefts.
4   The figure is based on the BCS sample risk grossed up to the England and Wales's population of those aged 16 or more.

Table 2.1 **Risks of phone theft for adults in 1999/2000, by offence type: British Crime Survey**

	Risks of phone thefts per 100 people aged 16 or more
Thefts from vehicles	0.29
Theft of personal property	0.23
Burglary	0.22
Theft from the person	0.18
Robbery	0.05

Note: The figures include attempts. Risks of personal property theft, theft from the person and robbery are based for those aged 16 or more. The other risks are for households. Not all offences are shown, where risks are very small. An average figure from the 2000 and 2001 BCS is taken.

The 'On Track' survey estimate

A series of school surveys was conducted as part of an evaluation of the 'On Track' component of the Crime Reduction Programme. The surveys covered 15,000 11–15 year olds in 29 secondary and 6 middle schools in England and Wales who were interviewed in June/July 2001.[5] Questions were specially included to cover phone theft victimisation of any kind.

The major shortcoming of the On Track survey is that the schools selected were from areas earmarked for special measures *because of* high deprivation levels. Thus, to the extent that victimisation levels are higher in poorer areas (and there is good reason to believe this is so), the On Track estimates will over-estimate the 'average' experience of school children.

This said, the results show an estimated 16 incidents of *actual* thefts per 100 in the sample – a very high figure.[6] A quarter of victims said they had more than one phone stolen in the last year – so the overall prevalence ('once or more' risk) risk was 11.9 per cent. If taken at face value, then, the On Track survey figures suggest that 11–15 year olds in England and Wales experienced 550,000 phone thefts between mid 2000 and mid 2001.[7]

Apart from the sample, there is also need to be cautious about the On Track figures because:

---

5   A paper and pencil self-completion questionnaire was used in all the school surveys. The results are provisional at the time of writing.
6   The children were asked whether they owned a phone or normally carried a phone. However, all children were asked the phone theft question, since some might not currently have a phone, but have had one before.
7   The population figures for the age group are for mid-2000.

- There were indications from the survey responses that some pupils may not have read the mobile phone questions carefully enough as referring to 'the last year'.

- There may have been a degree of exaggeration. Phone theft targeted at young victims had been much in the news and some children may have wanted to 'jump on the bandwagon'.

The On Track survey did not ask what types of phone thefts were involved. It did, however, ask victims whether they were using the phone at the time, and 14 per cent said they were. Incidents where this was the case would probably count as robberies. They were also asked whether they had the phone in their possession (28% did). Some of these might also have been robberies or thefts from the person – although the question is perhaps slightly ambiguous as regards whether the phone was actually taken from the youngster directly. With the caveats above, then, the results indicate that there were more than 6 incidents per 100 youngsters that were possibly robberies or thefts from the person – very greatly in excess of the BCS figure of 0.23 for adults.

The MORI survey

A survey done by MORI for the Youth Justice Board early in 2001 asked a similar question about general phone theft victimisation of just over 5,000 11–16 year olds. Although smaller in scale (and therefore with larger sampling error), the sample was more representative. The results showed a lower 5.0 per cent who said they had a phone actually stolen at least once in the last year – less than half the level in the On Track survey (11.9%).[8] Grossed up, then, the MORI survey indicates that about 200,000 11–16 year olds were victim at least once of a phone theft in 2000. (The MORI survey did not ask any questions about the circumstances of the theft.)

The burden of these survey results is that:

- Risks of phone theft seem much higher – indeed exceptionally high – for those at school. Even the lower estimate from the MORI survey is well in excess of the BCS estimate for adults, while the On Track survey gives a figure roughly double that from MORI. On the face of it, the risks for 11–16 year olds seem at least *five times* higher than for adults.

8   The rate for phone owners would be higher, though the MORI survey did not ask specifically about ownership. Nor did it ask about the number of times a phone was stolen.

- The On Track survey shows an even greater differential between adults and youngsters as regards phone thefts that probably involved robbery or theft from the person.

Estimates from six police forces

Information was collected from six police forces on the number of thefts involving mobile phones.[9] Three of these were non-metropolitan forces – Lancashire, Avon & Somerset, and Kent. Three were metropolitan forces – Greater Manchester Police (GMP), the West Midlands, and the Metropolitan Police District (MPD).

Risks
The number of phone thefts per head of population is shown in Figure 2.1. These are spread across a number of different offences (see Section 3). Risks differed across the six forces, with the highest per capita risks in the metropolitan forces. London had nearly double the risk of any other force. A national average is also shown. There are very few international figures available, but Briscoe (2001) gives figures for New South Wales that show a risk of much the same order.[10]

Figure 2.1   Risks of phone thefts per 100,000 population in six forces

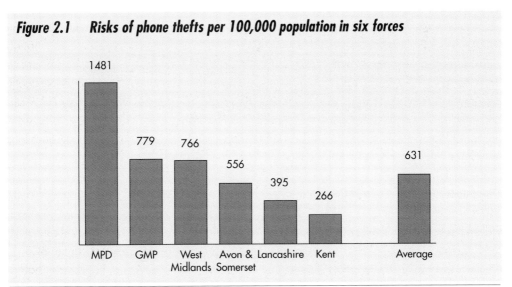

9   With the exception of the MPD, all force figures relate specifically to mobile phones stolen. In the MPD, the category was 'telecommunications equipment' for all periods except January – March 2001, when a special 'mobile phone' category was introduced.

10 The figures are for October 1999 to September 2000. The risk was 620 thefts per 100,000 population. In England and Wales, the estimated risk was 451 in 1999/00 and 631 in 2000/01 – which averages at 541.

The estimated number of recorded phone thefts

Across the six forces, an average of 6 per cent of all recorded crimes in 2000/01 involved phones. The average was 5 per cent in non-metropolitan forces, and 9 per cent in metropolitan ones. Extrapolating to England and Wales gives an estimated 330,000 offences involving phones recorded by the police. (These are both phones actually stolen as well as attempts to steal.)

The extrapolation procedure

The estimate of 330,000 offences is derived from applying the percentage of offences involving phones in the sampled forces to the total amount of recorded crime in England and Wales. Account has been taken of the differing proportion of phone thefts in metropolitan and non-metropolitan forces, as well as the different proportions of metropolitan and non-metropolitan forces sampled. (Weighting is done within each of the metropolitan and non-metropolitan forces sectors.) As a relatively small sample of non-metropolitan forces provided information, the extrapolated national average needs to be treated with caution.

Similar extrapolation procedures are mainly followed in Sections 3, 4 and 5. The number of forces on which extrapolation is based varies by topic, however. In Section 6 (offenders), and Section 7 (victims), a different averaging procedure has been followed. Here, the figures for each force or BCU providing information have been summed together.

False allegations

Another caveat about the police force estimates concerns the idea that some offences recorded may in fact actually be 'lost' phones reported as thefts because many insurance policies cover only theft not loss. Other people may report phones as stolen to try and move onto another contract giving a better phone or lower rates (known among operators as 'churning').

Although in some quarters much is made of the inflationary effect of 'false allegations', its extent is uncertain. 'Churning' will only apply to those on contracts (now a small minority). More important is that phone insurance coverage is very low as annual premiums are high relative to the cost of running a phone. Some household insurance policies may cover phone theft, but not all do, and any 'excess' applying will mean many claims are not worthwhile.

Nonetheless, two items of evidence are worth reporting, though the first is fragile and rather inconclusive.

- A police officer in Lewisham conducted a small exercise looking at reports of robberies in which a mobile phone was said to be the only item stolen. (He took reports at the 'front desk' only.) They were investigated against a range of factors including the gap between the date when the 'robbery' was said to have taken place and the date it was reported. On the basis of this gap together with other evidence, the officer concluded that 7 percent of losses were 'bogus' claims.

  Analysis of the current information on phone robberies (not all phone thefts) from the BCUs was at odds with the Lewisham results, however. Virtually all incidents were reported on the day victims said the offence took place, or the next day. This does not of course indicate they were 'true' allegations, Indeed, it seems likely that victims making false ones would claim the theft was very recent. (Saying it was some time ago might alert suspicion.)

- BT Cellnet undertook an exercise looking at all insurance claims for replacement phones due to theft made over a ten-week period in 2001. Cellnet checked the IMEI (International Mobile Equipment Identity) number to see whether it matched the type of phone for which a claim was being made. Call patterns of the phone were also monitored after the insurance claim was lodged. Cellnet concluded that a full 60 per cent of theft claims were false, weighted towards claims made for allegedly high value models. (When claimants were challenged, they said either they had made a mistake about the model, or they had now found the phone).

The high figure of false claims from the BT Cellnet exercise is salutary, but needs to be taken in tandem with insurance figures. Assuming that 10 per cent of owners were covered by insurance and chose to make a claim, and that 60% of these were false, then the estimated figure of 330,000 phone thefts recorded by the police would reduce by 6 per cent to just over 310,000. If insurance and false claim percentages were halved, the reduction would be 1.5 per cent, down to 325,00 offences. In sum, then, false allegations are likely to occur, difficult to assess, but probably of less importance than is sometimes supposed.

3.   Features of phone thefts

In this section, we look first at the frequency of phone theft. The first way to do this is to see which crimes generate the most, bearing in mind that some offences (thefts from cars, for example) are much more numerous than others (robbery, for example). Thus, the former could generate more phone thefts in numerical terms, even if the proportion of thefts from cars involving phones is smaller. The second approach is to compare the proportion of different offences that involve phones, disregarding the number of offences they generate. Information on both approaches comes from the BCS and from the police force figures – though the coverage of the two is not quite the same.

Which crimes generate the most thefts?

According to both police figures and the BCS, more mobile phones are stolen (or an attempt is made) in offences *other than robbery*.

The BCS
The BCS indicates that a third of phone thefts came from incidents classified in the BCS as miscellaneous thefts (Figure 3.1, with data from the 2001 and 2000 sweeps combined).[11] These cover unattended phones left in offices, leisure facilities, and on public transport etc. Nearly as many came from thefts from vehicles. Phones stolen in robbery made up 4 per cent of all offences, but the figure was much higher for thefts from the person (as explained, akin to robbery.)

Figure 3.1   *Percentage of all offences in which mobile phones are targeted against adults (2001 and 2000 BCS)*

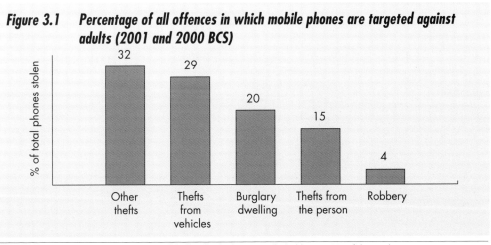

11 A few mobiles stolen in the course of thefts of vehicles are included here – 2% of the total.

Police figures

Information was available from four forces, relating to 2000/01.[12] The overall picture was somewhat similar to the BCS, although the actual proportions differed (Table 3.1). Thus, the force data showed that phones featured most in 'other' types of theft (i.e., those that are miscellaneous in nature), with the proportion in the force data (43%) greater than in the BCS (32%). This is not unexpected. The police figures, for instance, will include in 'other thefts' phones stolen by employees, as well as in shoplifting. Also, we know from the BCS that there are differences between offences in how often they are reported to the police. Thefts from vehicles, for instance, have a relatively low reporting rate. The next most common were phones taken in the course of thefts from cars, with the proportion here less than the BCS. Relatively low reporting rates may be a factor here.

The pattern was the same in each of the three years. Recent research in New South Wales, Australia has also found the same picture from police figures (Briscoe, 2001).

Table 3.1 Percentage of all offences in which mobile phones were most often targeted in 2000/01 (four police forces)

	MPD	West Midlands	GMP*	Avon and Somerset	Average**
	%	%	%	%	
Other theft	41	34	27	51	43
Theft from vehicles	14	19	20	22	18
Personal robbery	13	13	10*	7	10
Theft from the person	13	14	9	7	10
Burglary dwelling	9	13	21	10	11
Burglary other	5	5	12	4	5
Other offences ***	5	2	2	0	2
	100%	100%	100%	100%	100%
Total mobile phone thefts	**107,009**	**20,120**	**20,066**	**8,354**	

Notes:
*   The figure for GMP combines personal and commercial robbery.
**   The average is weighted by the relative size of the three metropolitan areas in the sample, as well as the relative contribution of all crime in metropolitan and non-metropolitan forces.
*** Other offences include commercial robberies.

12 For part of the period, the MPD gave figures for telecommunications equipment and these may include items other than mobile phones – e.g., ordinary phones, cordless phones, pay phones, and fax machines. Such items might be stolen in burglaries and commercial robberies. In personal robberies they are unlikely to feature much. Data from the West Midlands for 2000/01 shows that mobile phone thefts made up 96% of all stolen telecommunications equipment in personal robberies and 76% in commercial robberies. The pattern was similar for each year: 1999/00, 95% and 85% respectively and for 1998/999 89 per cent and 78%.

There was some variation by force, though there is no obvious explanation. For instance, half of phone thefts (and attempts) in Avon & Somerset came from miscellaneous thefts, but the figures were lower in the three metropolitan forces.

On average, 10 per cent of phones were targeted in the course of personal robberies – about third or fourth in importance in quantitative terms. The figure was the same for thefts from the person.[13]

Which offences involve phones most in proportionate terms

The perspective here is on which types of offence involve phone thefts most in proportionate terms.

The BCS

Figure 3.2 shows the BCS results (based on the 2001 and 2000 sweeps). Thefts from the person and other thefts most often involved a phone (11% of each). The figures for other offences, including robbery, were not much different, except that phones were stolen least often in the numerically large category of thefts from vehicles. (Attempts are included throughout.)

Figure 3.2 Proportion of each offence type involving a phone theft: 2001 and 2000 BCS

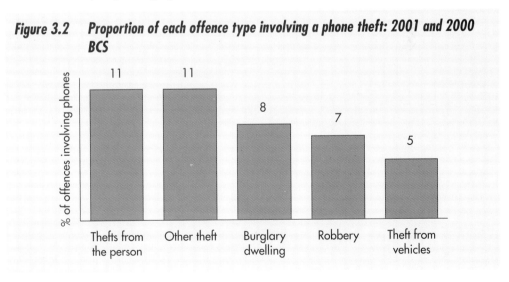

---

13 A few phones were taken in commercial robberies, but these offences are small in number compared to personal robberies.

Police figures

Figure 3.3 shows the picture for the MPD and for the other three forces combined.[14] The MPD is singled out as its pattern differed: in all but one type of offence there were more phones targeted in the MPD. This may be because higher phone ownership levels in the South East mean more phones are exposed to theft.[15] In the MPD, a full four in ten (39%) personal robberies involved the theft of a phone, and 23% in the other forces.

Figure 3.3 *Proportion of each offence type involving a phone theft in 2000/01: the MPD and three other forces*

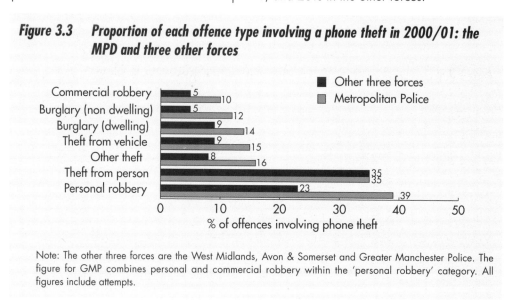

Note: The other three forces are the West Midlands, Avon & Somerset and Greater Manchester Police. The figure for GMP combines personal and commercial robbery within the 'personal robbery' category. All figures include attempts.

These proportions from police figures are higher than from the BCS, with the most marked differences for robbery and thefts from the person. Three factors may be at issue:

- The BCS excludes young victims which could affect the robbery and theft from the person figures in particular.

- Thefts involving phones are more likely to be reported to the police.[16]

- Some 'thefts' said to involve robbery or theft from the person could be false allegations (see Section 2).

14 Full details are in Table A3.1 in Appendix A. There were a few other offences in which phones were said to have been stolen – for example, violence against the person, fraud and forgery, and even sexual offences. The numbers, however, are very small.

15 Industry figures indicate that phone call traffic is higher than elsewhere within the M25, and in central London in particular.

16 Figures from the BCS indicate that about two-thirds of offences in which a phone was targeted were reported, but less than half of other offences. BCS figures are rather too fragile to give estimates of the reporting rates for particular offences. The On Track survey indicated that a third of young people who had a phone stolen reported it to the police.

Robbery

Robbery in general is an offence more concentrated in metropolitan forces than is the case for other offences. The per capita all robbery risk in the MPD is the highest, with risks next highest in the West Midlands and Greater Manchester. The proportion of phone robberies also tended to be higher in the metropolitan forces sampled, so differential risks of phone robbery are even more pronounced. Figure 3.4 shows results (based on personal and commercial robberies).

Figure 3.4   Risks of phone robbery per 100,000 population in six forces

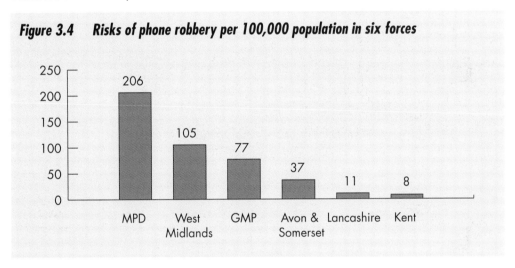

The concentration of phone robberies in city centres

Within metropolitan areas, the proportion of robberies involving phones is higher in city centre areas than elsewhere. This is evident from a comparison of force phone robberies (personal and commercial) and those in the BCU areas.[17] Figure 3.5 shows the BCUs set alongside the force within which they were located (e.g., Westminster next to the MPD). In each BCU, the proportion of robberies that involved phones was higher than the respective force figure. On average, 38% of robberies were phone-related in the four BCUs.

---

17 To do this for the BCUs involves applying the percentage of robberies that were phone-related according to the sample of early 2001 cases to the BCU total annual robbery figures. These are now reported in the routine Statistical Bulletin on recorded crime (see Povey et al., 2001). The BCU estimates, then, are cautious ones.

Figure 3.5 Percentage of robberies involving phones in BCUs and forces, 2000-01

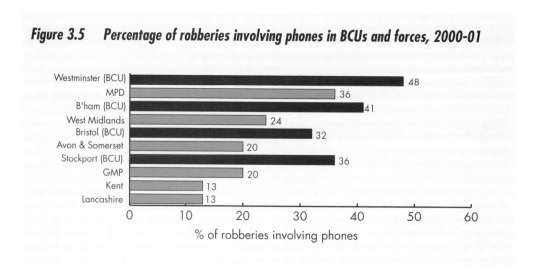

These results, then, strongly indicate that robbery in city centres is more likely to involve phones than is the case in the force as a whole. This may be because the types of offenders in the business of stealing phones (even if along with other things) may frequent city centres themselves more. Busy central areas may also provide the easiest pickings from other young socialites or busy shoppers.

Phone-only robberies and those in which other items are taken

Forces

Figures from three forces are available for 2000/01 on how robberies break down.[18] These indicate that just over a third of *phone* robberies involved *only* a phone. In terms of *all* robberies, phone only robberies accounted for about 8 per cent.

BCUs

Information collected in the four city centre BCUs showed a similar average of a third of *phone* robberies involving *only* a phone.[19] However, the results varied between BCUs. In Westminster, 40% of phone robberies only involved a phone, while the figure in Bristol was 26% (Table 3.2).

18 The forces were the West Midlands, Avon & Somerset and GMP. The figures for Avon & Somerset relate to personal robberies only. Those for other forces relate to personal and commercial robberies, but as the number of commercial robberies is relatively very small, the results would be very similar on the basis of personal robberies alone.

19 The comparison with the force data is not exact. The BCU information also covered incidents in which a phone was asked for, but not stolen. In these cases, it is not possible to say whether it was *only* the phone that was asked for. Table 3.2 shows the details. The assumption is made that where a phone was asked for, other items were too.

In terms of *all robberies*, an average of 13% involved only a phone in the BCUs– higher than the average force figure (8%). The difference is not striking, but it may indicate that robberies in which phones are involved are rather different in nature in city centre areas than across a force generally.

Table 3.2 **Phone robberies at BCU level: personal and commercial robbery**

	Westminster %	B'ham %	Bristol %	Stockport %	Average %
Phone robberies					
Phone only item stolen	40	35	26	36	33
Additional items stolen	47	44	67	27	49
Phone asked for					
but not stolen	14	21	7	38	17
	100%	100%	100%	100%	100%
N phone robberies	96	80	119	64	
Phone only of all robberies*	19	15	8	13	13
N Total robberies	201	193	374	187	946

Notes: Columns may not total exactly 100% due to rounding.
* Assumes an incident in which a phone was asked for also includes other items being asked for.

4.   Trends in phone thefts overall

The results in this section show a substantial growth in offences involving the theft of phones. A key issue is whether this is because phones are being specifically targeted. It could, of course, be that phones are one of a number of 'stealable' items, and their increasing appearance in thefts reflects greater ownership. This point is returned to in Section 5.

The BCS

Table 4.1 shows results from the last four sweeps of the BCS. In 2000, there were 16% more phones stolen (or attempted to be stolen) than in 1999, and a full 190% more than in 1995. The proportion of all incidents in which a phone was targeted (albeit often along with other property) was 5.5 per cent in 2000: i.e., about one in 20. This is similar to the 6 per cent estimated on the basis of six forces' figures.

Table 4.1   British Crime Survey estimates of mobile phone thefts (those aged 16 or more)

	1995	1997	1999	2000
Mobile phones stolen 1	160,000	270,000	400,000	470,000
% of all thefts	1.1%	2.6%	4.0%	5.5%

1   Based on risk figures grossed up to the population of England and Wales aged 16 or more. The risks relate to incidents in which a phone was stolen or an attempt was made.

The BCS increase in thefts is less since 1995 (at 190%) than the increase in phone subscribers (which was virtually 600% – see Figure 1.1). Nonetheless, some of the increase in thefts will, of course, reflect increased ownership, and this is taken up in Section 5.

Police figures

Figures were available from six police forces as to the total number of phone thefts over the past three years. These can be set against the total amount of recorded crime in each force to see how the percentage of all crime that involved mobile phones has changed recently. (Kent provided figures for the last four years.) Table 4.2 also gives an average figure for England and Wales as a whole, extrapolated from the sampled forces.

In each police force, the number of phone thefts has at least doubled in two years – i.e., between 1998/999 and 2000/01. There was a higher (three-fold) increase in the West Midlands and Lancashire. Coupled with this, the proportion of total crime that was phone-related rose in each area over the two years – both because of the higher increase in the number of phone thefts, and the fall in other offences in some forces. In 1998/99, phones were stolen in only 1–2 per cent of all crime in all forces except the MPD (5 per cent). By 2000/01, phones were stolen in 3–6 per cent of all crimes outside the MPD, and 11% within it. (See Table 4.2 opposite.)

The BCS results suggested a continuing rise in phone thefts between 1999 and 2000, albeit with some degree of uncertainty due to sampling error. The police figures, in contrast, indicate that the rise in incidents involving phones peaked between 1998/999 and 1999/00 and fell somewhat between 1999/00 and 2000/01. For example, in the West Midlands, phone thefts more than doubled between the first two years, while the percentage change was thereafter less than half this, at 45%. The average figures indicate a 65% increase in phone thefts between 1998/99 and 1999/2000, and a smaller 41% increase over the last two years.

Figure 4.1 illustrates the possible peaking in the rate of increase in phone thefts earlier than 2000/01. (Kent provided data since 1997/98).[20]

Figure 4.1   Percentage increase in thefts involving phones in six police forces

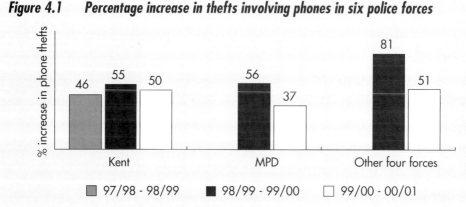

Note. The four forces are the West Midlands, Avon & Somerset, GMP, and Lancashire
Their figures are combined to produce the average.

---

20 Full details are in Table A4.1 in Appendix A.

Table 4.2 Growth of all recorded offences involving phones, six forces

	Total crimes N (000s)	% change in total crime since previous year	% of all crime involving phone thefts	Phone thefts N (000s)	% change in phone thefts since previous year
MPD *					
98/99	934		5	50.4	
99/00	1,017	9	8	78.4	56
00/01	994	-2	11	107.0	37
West Midlands					
98/99	315		2	6.6	
99/00	365	16	4	13.9	110
00/01	365	0	6	20.1	45
Avon and Somerset					
98/99	150		2	3.5	
99/00	147	-2	4	5.8	65
00/01	149	1	6	8.4	44
GMP					
98/99	362		2	7.9	
99/00	377	4	3	13.0	64
00/01	363	-4	6	20.1	55
Lancashire					
98/99	118		1	1.7	
99/00	109	-8	3	3.2	84
00/01	118	8	5	5.6	74
Kent **					
98/99	129		1	1.8	
99/00	125	-3	2	2.8	55
00/01	128	3	3	4.2	50
Average ***				Estimated	
98/99	5,109		3	143.1	
99/00	5,301	4	4	236.2	65
00/01	5,171	-2	6	332.4	41

Notes:

* Figures for MPD for 2000/01 are based on revised boundary changes.

** Kent figures exclude mobile phone accessories. The overall number of crimes in Kent in 1997/8 has been adjusted for comparability to take account of the change in counting rules.

*** The average change in crime is for England and Wales. The other average figures take account of the share of crime in the sampled metropolitan and non-metropolitan forces relative to metropolitan and non-metropolitan forces as a whole. The average is weighted within these two sectors.

Percentage changes are calculated on unrounded figures.

This section looks in more detail at trends in phone robberies. It draws only on police information. BCS estimates of phone robberies over time are not reliable enough to take as an indication of trends.[21] Some reference is also made to police figures on thefts from the person. These are related in nature to robbery, and as seen generate rather more phone thefts than robbery according to the BCS, and the same proportion according to police figures.

The emphasis of this section is on how far one can say that phones have fuelled the recent rise in robbery. First, a number of pointers are drawn from figures over the past three years:

- The increase in the proportion of robberies involving phones.

- The thus bigger increase in phone robberies relative to other offences involving phones.

- National figures showing that personal robberies have increased more than commercial robberies.

- The higher increase in *phone* robberies that involve *only* a phone, as opposed to those that involved a phone and other items.

These pointers taken together certainly suggest that phones have played a part in the recent rise in robbery. The section ends, though, by looking at robbery trends over the 1990s as a whole – bearing in mind that phones were unlikely to have been implicated in the rise in robbery in the early 1990s. It also illustrates the more recent trend in robbery *excluding* phone-only incidents and discusses knowing for certain how far recent *all* robbery figures are fuelled by phone theft.

Changes in the proportion of robberies involving phones

Information was available from six forces for the last three years on the proportion of robberies that involved phone theft. Figure 5.1 looks at all six forces. An average is also shown, which is heavily influenced by the preponderance of robbery in the MPD.[22]

---

21 Robbery of any type is fairly unusual (only 0.5 per cent were victims in 1999), and so sampling error is large.
22 The average again takes account of the share of robbery in metropolitan and non-metropolitan areas in the sampled forces, and is weighted within these two sectors. Of all robberies in England and Wales in 2000/01, 43% took place in the MPD.

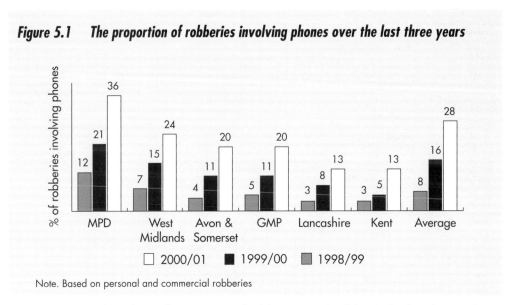

Figure 5.1   The proportion of robberies involving phones over the last three years

Note. Based on personal and commercial robberies

In 1998/99, a relatively small proportion of robberies involved the theft of a phone – 8 per cent on average (an estimated 5,500). The proportion was most significant in the MPD at the time (12%). By 2000/01, the proportion had increased markedly in each force, and was as high as 36% in the MPD.

The picture is not dissimilar for thefts from the person. In 1998/99, 15% of these offences on average involved a phone – higher than the 8 per cent for robbery (see above). By 2000/01, the proportion had increased markedly to 33% – again higher than for robbery.[23]

The change in phone robberies relative to other offences

According to four forces providing data, there has been a bigger percentage increase in phone robberies relative to other offences involving phones between 1998/99 and 2000/01, and in most by some margin (Figure 5.2).

---

23 Tables A4.2 and A5.1 in Appendix A shows the details by force.

Figure 5.2   Percentage change in phone thefts for each offence type: 1998/99–2000/01

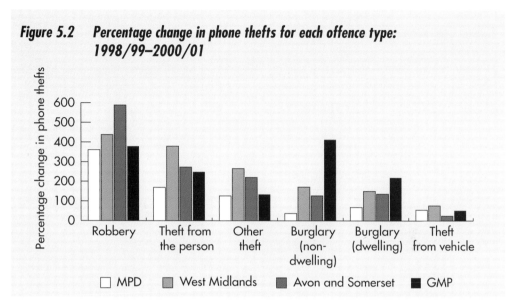

In Avon and Somerset, there was nearly a 600% increase in personal robberies involving phones between 1998/99 and 2000/01, although on average *all* phone thefts little more than doubled. Similarly, in the three other forces there was a rough 400% increase in phone-related personal robberies, although the percentage change for *all* phone thefts ranged between 100% and 200%.

Thefts from the person involving phones have increased less than phone robberies but still more than other phone thefts. This suggests that the targeting of phones in 'acquisitive street crime' has become more of a problem than in relation to other non-contact crimes such as burglary. Nonetheless, the smaller rise over the two years in thefts from the person underscores the particular growth in robbery *per se*.

To the extent that false allegations made with respect to robbery and theft from the person specifically have increased over time more than false allegations in relation to other phone thefts, then the bigger increases could be overstated.

(It is interesting that the smallest percentage change was in relation to thefts from vehicles, and this has also applied in Australia (Briscoe, 2001). It may be that improved car security has curbed opportunities for stealing phones from cars. Or it may be that as mobile phone use has escalated, owners are less likely to want to leave them behind.)

Personal and commercial robberies

Since 1998/99, national robbery figures have been broken down into personal and commercial (or business) robberies. Figure 5.3 shows that personal robberies have increased much more over the past two years than commercial robberies.

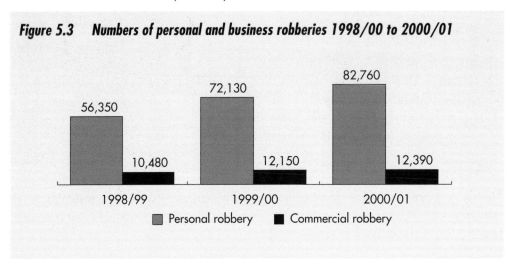

Figure 5.3   Numbers of personal and business robberies 1998/00 to 2000/01

The rate of increase between 1998/99 and 1999/00 was higher (at 28%) than between 1999/00 and 2000/01 (15%), which mirrors the picture for all phone thefts.

The growth in phone robberies involving only a phone

Information was provided by three forces on the respective growth in 'phone-only' robberies, as against phone robberies in which phones are stolen along with other items.[24] It shows a higher increase in the former than the latter (Figure 5.4).[25]

---

24 The forces were the West Midlands, Avon & Somerset, and GMP. They relate to personal robberies with the exception of the GMP.
25 Table A5.2 has details for each force.

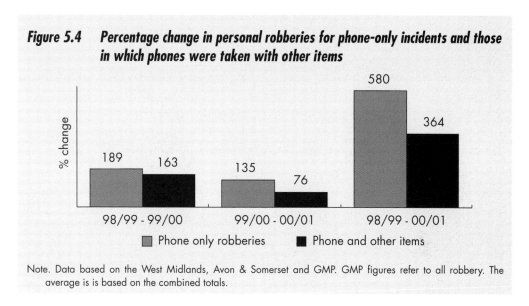

Figure 5.4   Percentage change in personal robberies for phone-only incidents and those in which phones were taken with other items

Note. Data based on the West Midlands, Avon & Somerset and GMP. GMP figures refer to all robbery. The average is is based on the combined totals.

Nonetheless, the proportion *of all* robberies which relates to phone-only incidents is still relatively small for the three forces: 8 per cent in 2000/01, 4 per cent in the previous year, and 2 per cent in the year before that.

The effect of phone robbery on the increase in robbery offences

The information above all points in the direction of phones having a part to play in the recent rise in robbery. Why it does not conclusively prove it is taken up at the end of the section. First, though, we examine robbery trends over the 1990s as a whole, as well as the shorter time span for which more detailed force figures have been collected.

Trends over the 1990s

Figure 5.5 compares the picture for robbery with that for all theft and handling offences – a proxy for all crime.[26] (Because of the markedly different number of offences involved, separate axes are used.) Two main points emerge.

- First, the robbery trend has had a different dynamic from thefts. Thefts peaked in 1993, since when they have fallen. Police-recorded robberies, in contrast, increased in every year since 1990 except 1997/8 – when there was a general fall in most crime. The increase in robbery in 1999/00 was the highest in the 1990s.[27]

---

26 Theft and handling form a large proportion of all crimes recorded, and the trend in them is less affected by the changes to the police counting rules that occurred in 1998/9.

27 The increase (7%) between 1998/99 and the previous year is slightly inflated due to the introduction of new counting rules for recorded crime.

- Second, whatever caused the increases in robberies in the early to mid-1990s, it was unlikely to be mobile phones. Ownership levels did not start to reach appreciable levels until after the mid-1990s and most phones early on were held on contract (and therefore more likely to be blocked if stolen). Ownership by young people was also low. The trend in thefts from the person, incidentally, has been generally similar to robbery, with an increase of about 190% since 1990 – rather more than robbery (160%).

Figure 5.5 *Trends in robbery and theft and handling offences recorded by the police since 1990*

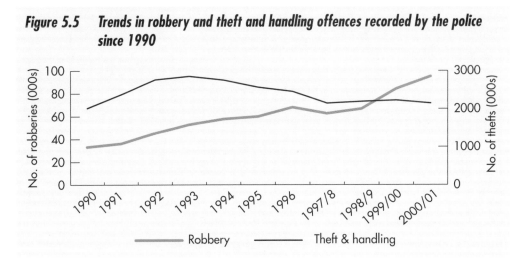

Force figures for 2000/01 compared with 1998/99

A more direct test as regards phone robberies is information from six forces relating to phone and non-phone robberies over the past three years. Table 5.1 shows the results, comparing figures for 1998/99 with those for 2000/01 – a two-year gap. (The figures relate to personal and commercial robberies combined.)

The increase in *phone* robberies was substantial in all forces – much greater than for robbery as a whole. If phone robberies are subtracted from the robbery total, this has the effect of greatly reducing the robbery rise in all forces, down from an average rise of 42% in *all* robberies over the two years, to an estimated 12% (the last column of the table). As mentioned before, though, the sample of forces included here is relatively modest, so the average figures are cautious ones. There are also other caveats about the subtraction of phone robberies which are discussed later.

Table 5.1   **Robbery and phone robbery trends between 1998/999 and 2000/01**

	% increase for all robberies	% increase for phone robberies	% increase for non-phone robberies
MPD	56	361	13
Lancashire	25	492	12
Avon & Somerset	51	588	26
West Midlands	55	438	26
Kent	40	529	26
GMP	30	379	10
Average	42	377	12

Note: The average here takes account of the share of robbery in the sampled metropolitan and non-metropolitan forces relative to metropolitan and non-metropolitan forces as a whole. The average is weighted within these two sectors

In the last year (i.e., 2000/01 compared with 1999/2000) excluding phone robberies means that robberies *fell* in the MPD and stayed the same in the West Midlands. On the basis of an estimated average figure, then, robbery might have fallen nationally in the region of –3 per cent, instead of the 13% increase (see Table A5.1 in Appendix A).

Information from six forces over the past three years shows the increase in *phone* robberies was much greater than for robbery as a whole. Some part of the increase will be due simply to greater phone ownership. Some may also be due to more false allegations as a corollary of higher ownership. In addition some may be because there is more reporting to the police as phone ownership has grown in particular among youngsters for whom a phone will be a particularly valuable item.

The effect on the longer-term trend in robbery

The trend in robbery since 1990 can be re-drawn to account for these differential changes in phone and non-phone robberies. Essentially, the steps are as follows.

- Figures for phone and non-phone robberies over the past three years from six forces are extrapolated to England and Wales using average procedures already described.

- An estimate is made of the number of phone robberies in the three years prior to 1998/9. (The number is assumed to be fairly small.)

- The number of phone robberies is subtracted from the robbery total.

Figure 5.6 shows the results. The 'robbery-less-phone' trend is now much shallower, with a levelling off in the past two years. There are important qualifications, however. It would be unrealistic to see the 'robbery-less-phone' trend as a true indicator of what the situation might have been. This is because some of the robberies omitted may have taken place anyway. The fact that a phone was stolen may simply reflect the fact that they are now prominent among the smaller, higher value 'stealable' items that people carry on them. The offenders in Feltham, as it happened, were fairly unanimous in putting cash and jewellery as higher in importance than phones themselves. They also said that if these seemed hard to obtain, then making off with just a phone was fairly adequate recompense.

Figure 5.6 **Trends in robberies and theft and handling offences recorded by the police since 1990, with adjustment for phone robberies**

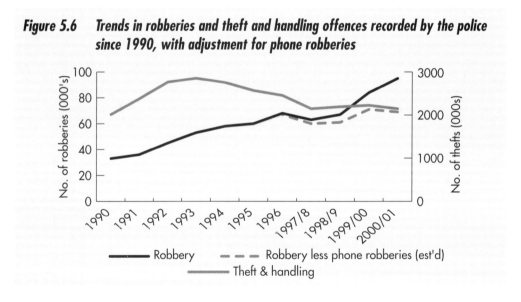

A more stringent test of what the overall robbery trend might have been is to exclude incidents in which only a phone was taken (constituting, as said, 8 per cent of all robberies in 2000/1). This is on the premise that phone-only incidents are more likely to be specifically due to phones than robberies where a phone was taken with other items. To do this involves estimation on the basis of only three forces that could provide three years of information on phone-only robberies.[28] The resulting estimates in Figure 5.7, then, are very tentative. The latest change in robberies excluding phone-only incidents is rather more favourable than all robberies (an 8% increase between 2000/01 and the year before, as against 13%), but less so than robberies with *all* phone incidents excluded.

Figure 5.7 **Trends in robberies recorded by the police since 1990, with adjustment for phone-only robberies**

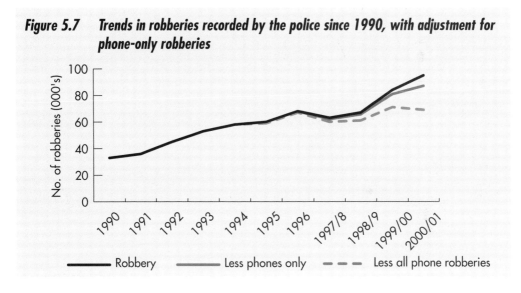

28 The proportion of *personal* robberies in the West Midlands and Avon and Somerset that were phone only incidents is applied to the total number of commercial and personal robberies. The three forces in the analysis accounted for 25% of the robberies in England and Wales.

6   Offenders in phone robberies

Data were provided by three police forces on persons accused of robberies involving the theft of a mobile phone ('phone robberies') over the 12 months April 2000 to March 2001.[29] Personal and commercial robberies were included, except for Avon & Somerset who provided figures for personal robberies only. Attempts were also included. The total number of accused in each force varied from under one hundred in Avon and Somerset to just over two thousand in the MPD.

RDS researchers also collected information on suspects in phone robberies that occurred over three months between January and March 2001. A sample of about 200 records was taken in each of four city centre Basic Command Units (BCUs).[30] These again covered personal and commercial robberies (attempted and actual) – although there were very few commercial incidents indeed. The BCU data also included information on incidents in which a phone was targeted although not actually stolen.

It should be borne in mind that the information on accused or suspects does not necessarily relate to *different* offenders. Some prolific offenders may be implicated in a number of different offences, and they will be counted once for each.

Gender of offenders

The overwhelming majority of offenders were male. The proportion of males was similar in each police force area. There was also relatively little variation in the BCUs, although the proportion of male suspects was rather higher than in the force accused data (Table 6.1). It may be that phone robbery in city centres is even more of a male pursuit than in other areas.

---

29 Figures for the MPD relate to phone and telecommunications equipment.
30 Details of suspects are based on arrest data if the suspect was apprehended. If not, victims/witnesses statements were used. These will inevitably be based on their impressions, and this should be borne in mind.

The dominance of male offenders is fully in line with offending patterns in general. In 1999, for instance, 90% or more of those cautioned and convicted for criminal damage, robbery, motoring offences, burglary and sexual offences were male (East and Campbell, 2001). In addition, in the latest sweep of the Youth Lifestyle Survey, males constituted approximately 80% of those aged 12–30 who said they had been cautioned or taken to court at least once in the last year (Flood-Page et al., 2000).[31] The MORI survey for the Youth Justice Board (MORI, 2001) also found that boys were more likely to have stolen a phone than girls (2 per cent versus 1 per cent respectively) although the differential is less marked than that within the sampled forces and BCUs.

Table 6.1   Gender of those involved in phone robberies

	Male %	Female %	Total accused/ suspects
Force level (accused): 2000-1			
Metropolitan Police District	88	12	2020
West Midlands	89	11	727
Avon and Somerset	90	10	67
BCU level (suspects) between Jan and March 2001			
Westminster (MPD)	92	8	232
Birmingham (West Midlands)	93	7	196
Bristol (Avon & Somerset)	97	3	174
Stockport (GMP)	92	8	242

Note: Figures for the West Midlands are for persons' accused of personal and commercial robbery that included the theft of a mobile phone. Figures for the Metropolitan Police District are for persons accused of personal and commercial robbery of telephone equipment or mobile phones. Avon and Somerset provided information on personal robberies only.

---

31 The Youth Lifestyle Survey was conducted in 1998/9 and is a self-report offending survey of about 5,000 young people aged between twelve and thirty living in private households in England and Wales.

Age of offenders

The accused

The accused information from police forces indicates that most of those involved in phone robbery were young. Figure 6.1 shows the proportion of offenders at each age up to the age of 24. Figures for the three forces are combined. Because the MPD has by far the largest number, the combined average will be heavily influenced by its pattern.

The peak age of those accused of phone robbery was 16, with 16 year olds constituting 18% of all offenders. Those aged 15 were also over-represented, making a third of all offenders aged 15 or 16. Those over the age of 24 constituted only 10 per cent of offenders. Only 1 per cent were aged 40 or more.

Figure 6.1   The age of offenders for the combined forces of MPD, West Midlands and Avon and Somerset

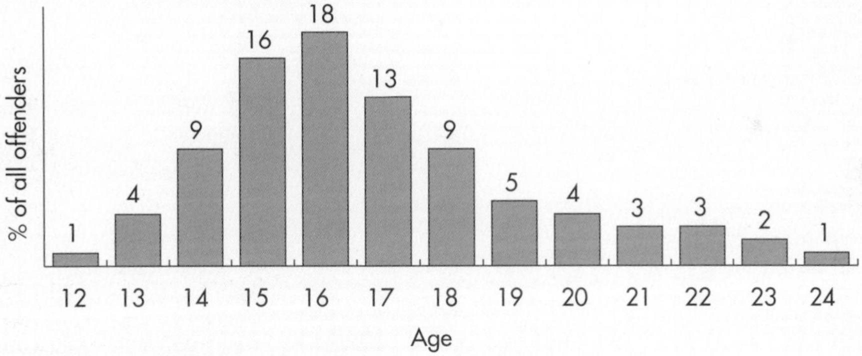

Note: The base is all offenders, including those over the age of 24.

The age profile reflects that of male offenders, who are in the majority. The number of females was relatively small (n = 321) so any differences are tentative. The indications are, though, that females accused of phone robbery are rather younger than males. All told, 79% of females were under 18, compared with 61% for males.

Variations by force

Those accused of phone robbery seemed particularly young in the MPD (Table 6.2). Among males, 65% were under 18, and a full 81% of girls.[32]

---

32 Further details can also be found in Table A6.1 in Appendix A.

Table 6.2   Age of accused: percentage of all those accused (police force information)

	10-13 %	14-17 %	All under 18 %	Total N (all offenders, 100%)
Metropolitan Police District				
Total	7	60	67	2020
Males	6	59	65	1783
Females	15	66	81	237
West Midlands				
Total	4	48	52	723
Males	5	45	50	646
Females	3	69	71	77
Avon and Somerset				
Total	3	42	45	67
Males	3	38	42	60
Average				
Total	6	56	63	2810
Males	6	55	61	2489
Females	12	67	79	321

Note: Averages are based on the combined total number of offenders in the three forces, which means that MPD will have the greatest affect on the average figure. The number of females in Avon and Somerset is too small to analyse by age.

Suspects

Suspects tended to be slightly older than those accused of phone robbery (Table A6.2 in Appendix A). This may be because they look older than they actually are to their victims. It might also be that older offenders are less likely to be apprehended. The average proportion of suspects under 18 was 55% as against 63% from the force figures on those accused.[33]

The proportion of young suspects was by far the lowest in Bristol (28%), somewhat echoing the picture from the Avon and Somerset force. It was by far the highest in Stockport (71%). This illustrates the diverse nature of phone robbery.

---

33 There were two suspects aged under 10 – both from Birmingham (a boy and girl). As those under 10 are below the age of criminal responsibility, they would not appear in accused data.

There were relatively few female suspects (n=55), and so reliable conclusions are again difficult. The indications are though that, as with the accused results, a greater proportion of female suspects were under 18 than males (Westminster was an exception). Table A6.2 in Appendix A has details.

The age profile of phone robbers compared with other offenders

Robbery in general seems an offence weighted more towards the young than other offences. Of those cautioned and convicted in England and Wales in 1999 for instance, 38% were under 18 for burglary, 30% for theft and handling offences, but 42% for robbery.

The BCU information allows a comparison of the age profile of those suspected of phone and non-phone robberies. Compared with the half (56%) of the phone robbery suspects who were under 18, the figure was much lower (31%) for suspects in other robberies (Figure 6.2).[34]

Figure 6.2   Age of phone robbery and non-phone robbery suspects: BCU information

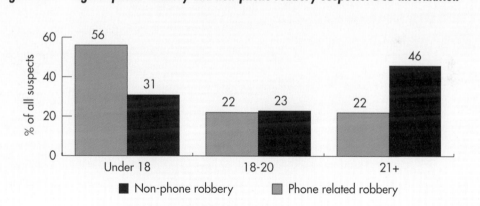

---

34 There was less difference for females: 62% of suspects in phone robberies were under 18, and 54% of other robbery suspects.

Ethnicity

To put the findings on the ethnicity in proper context, one needs to account for the proportion of minority ethnic groups in the *total* population in different areas. Figures from the Office for National Statistics give the breakdown for the three force areas, as well as for Greater Manchester, for which there is only BCU suspect information (Table 6.3). The breakdown of population in the central areas of Westminster, Birmingham, Bristol and Stockport may well be different again, although no figures are available on this. Also, the ethnic composition of the *younger* population in different areas is likely to be less heavily weighted to whites.

Table 6.3   *Ethnic breakdown of force populations*

	White %	Black %	Asian %	Other %
Metropolitan Police	82	8	6	4
West Midlands	87	3	9	1
Avon & Somerset	98	1	1	1
Greater Manchester	94	1	4	1

Notes.   Figures are based on mid-1999 population estimates for those aged 10 and over. Black includes mixed origin. 'Other' includes Chinese. Source: Home Office (2000).

The accused

According to the three forces supplying data, the majority of those accused of phone robbery were black in the MPD and the West Midlands (Figure 6.3).[35] In the MPD, they accounted for a full 71% of those accused. Both forces have larger black populations, but the disparity in the ethnic composition of those accused is nonetheless marked.

---

35 There were differences in coding of ethnicity, with some forces and BCUs using four or five categories and others six. For present purposes, Whites are White and Dark European; Blacks are Afro-Caribbean and 'blacks'; Asians are those from the Indian sub-continent; and others are Arab, Egyptian, Chinese, Japanese and those of mixed origin.

Figure 6.3   Those accused of phone robbery, by ethnicity (police force information)

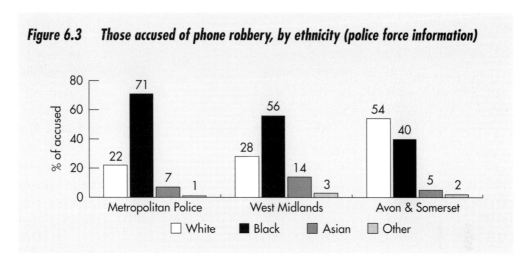

Ethnicity of suspects

On the whole, the ethnicity of suspects was similar to that of the accused – the majority being non-white in three of the four BCUs (Figure 6.4 and Table A6.3 in Appendix A).

Figure 6.4   Those suspected of phone robbery, by ethnicity (BCU information)

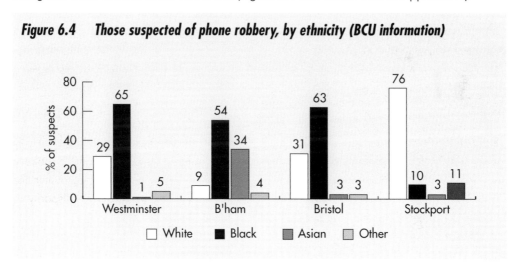

There were some differences according to area. The main features are:

- In Westminster, 65% of suspects were black – slightly lower than for the MPD as a whole. Asians made up a slightly lower proportion of suspects than in the force accused data.

- In Birmingham, a similar proportion of suspects were black as in the West Midlands force as a whole. In the city centre, Asians featured more as suspects (34% of suspects were Asian) than they did in the force as a whole. This figure was well in excess of any other BCU.

- In Bristol, blacks made up a greater proportion of suspects (63%) than in the force as a whole – and it was not far behind Westminster.

- In Stockport, the majority of suspects were white. The 'other' group was also high compared with the other localities. Police coding practices may be an issue here.

Lone or multiple suspects

From the BCU records it was possible to examine other features of what happened in cases of phone robbery, including the number of offenders involved in an incident.

Offenders most often operated with others: more than two-thirds (69%) of incidents on average involved offenders working in groups of two or more. For these, the split was fairly even between offenders operating in pairs and in groups of more than two. (There were quite a number of incidents (14%) in which five or more offenders were involved.)

There was some variation across area, however (Figure 6.5). In Bristol, the split between group and lone offenders was more equal. In Stockport, phone robbery was more often a group activity. The dominance of white offenders here seems to underlie this, since whites were more likely to act in groups (see below).[36]

---

36 In fact all ethnic groups in Stockport were more likely to offend with others. However, the sample in Stockport for groups other than whites was small – there were only six blacks, one Asian and six 'other' suspects.

Figure 6.5   Lone and multiple suspects (BCU information)

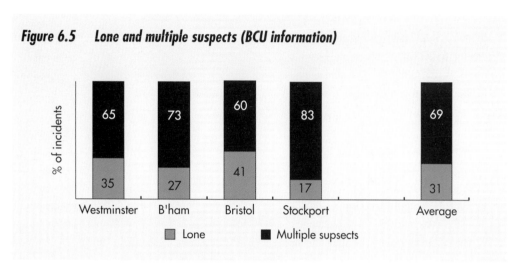

Other research has also found that the majority of offences are committed by offenders operating with others. In a survey of male prisoners in 34 prisons across England and Wales during April and May 2000, more than half who had committed crimes such as thefts of and from cars, and burglary, had done so with others at least occasionally (Lewis and Mhlanga, 2001).

More pertinent is whether phone robbery was more often committed in groups than other types of robbery. The BCU information suggests this is the case. The pattern held in each BCU (Figure 6.6).

Figure 6.6   Multiple suspects in phone and non-phone robberies (BCU information)

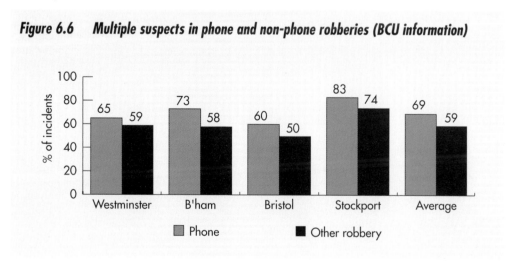

There are some other differences worth noting. The points below relate to the average picture for the BCUs.

- **Gender**. Keeping small numbers in mind, it appears that slightly more females acted in groups (74%) than males (69%).[37]

- **Age**. More of those aged under 18 (80%) worked with others than did older offenders (62%).[38]

- **Ethnicity**. Rather more whites than blacks acted with others (Figure 6.7). The biggest difference, though, was with regard to Asians, who seemed much more likely to offend with others – bearing the small number of incidents (N = 46) in mind.

Figure 6.7   Lone and group offending, by ethnicity (BCU information)

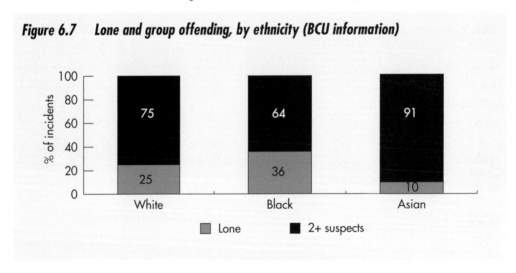

Victims of phone robbery

Information on victims of phone robbery was available from the same three forces as provided details on those accused. There was also partial information from four other forces: the Greater Manchester Police (GMP), Merseyside, Lancashire and Staffordshire.[39] GMP was able to provide some figures for the past three years. Victim information was also derived from incident records in the same four BCUs from which suspect information was collected. Most of the force and BCU information relates to both personal and commercial robberies.[40] Attempts are included.

Gender of victims

The majority of victims of phone robbery were male (Table 7.1). This was true both at police force and BCU level where, for instance, the average was 81% male. In London, rather more victims were female than elsewhere. The trend data from GMP indicates that the preponderance of male victims has remained stable over the last three years.

Table 7.1   The gender of victims in phone robberies

	Male %	Female %	Total victims where gender was given
Force level (2000/1)			
MPD	74	26	14,702
West Midlands	80	20	2,856
Avon and Somerset	77	23	557
GMP	83	17	1,954
Merseyside	79	21	99
Lancashire	78	22	153
BCU level (Jan-March 2001)			
Westminster	77	23	97
Birmingham	86	14	87
Bristol	77	23	124
Stockport	88	13	64

Note: Rows may not total 100% due to rounding.

---

39 Figures for Staffordshire only relate to the six-month period October 2000–April 2001. (Other force data are for April 2000–March 2001.) Figures are for victims of robberies involving the theft of a mobile phone (including offences where items other than a mobile phone were also stolen).
40 In Lancashire and Avon & Somerset, only victims of personal robbery are included.

The gender victim / suspect interaction

Given earlier results on the heavy preponderance of male *offenders*, it is clear that phone robbery is mainly a male-on-male activity. Table 7.2 shows the results.

Male-on-male incidents seem rather more common in relation to phone robberies than other robberies. The BCU information shows that 77% of the former involved only male suspects and male victims, while for other robberies the figure was 71%.[41]

Table 7.2   Offenders and victims: % of all incidents (BCU information)

	All phone robberies
Male offenders(s): male victim	77%
Male offenders(s): female victim	14%
Female offender(s): female victim	4%
Mixed group offenders: female victim	2%
Mixed group offenders: male victim	2%
Female offender(s): male victim	1%
	100%

The male-on-male feature of phone robbery is in line with what we know about other 'contact' crimes – at least those without a domestic element. Even so, one might imagine that females would be easier targets for phone robbery. According to the accounts of offenders in Feltham, though, choosing women was "out of order". This was not so much because they were an easier (and less 'macho') option, but more to do with notions about respecting women (the "weaker sex", as one offender put it). The higher proportion of male-on-male incidents in phone robberies suggests that these views may hold more strongly for some types of offence than others. The Feltham offenders also contested that young males were targeted because they were less likely to want to tell the police. How far this is true is difficult to say.

Female victims

Although most incidents against women were perpetrated by men, a third involved female offenders or mixed groups. These were very unusual when men were targeted. For instance, about a fifth of women were targeted by women alone, but only 1 per cent of male victims (Table 7.3). In addition 12% of female victims were targeted by groups of male and female offenders, but only 3 per cent of male victims.

41 Details are in Table A7.1, Appendix A.

Table 7.3   Gender differences in suspects and victims (BCU information)

	Male victim %	Female victim %	All victims %
Suspects involved:			
Single male suspect	27	48	31
More than one male suspect	69	20	59
Single female suspect	0	9	2
More than one female suspect	1	12	4
Group of male/female suspects	3	12	5
Total	100%	100%	100%

Age of victims

Figure 7.1 shows the age profile of victims combining the results from five forces and the four BCUs. Those under 18 constituted nearly half (48%) of all victims, with the peak at age 15 and 16. Those aged 18 to 29 constituted 39% of victims.

Figure 7.1   Age of victims as a percentage of all victims (combined force and BCU results)

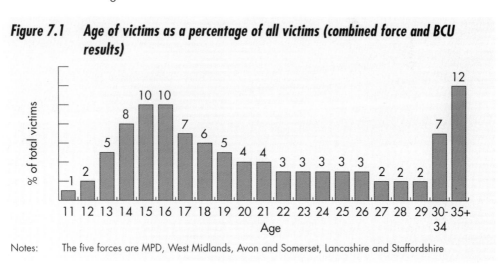

Notes: The five forces are MPD, West Midlands, Avon and Somerset, Lancashire and Staffordshire

The average was calculated by combining the number of victims in each force and BCU. The picture was not entirely the same in different areas. For instance, in Staffordshire there were more younger victims (54% under 18). In Stockport a full 80% were under 18 – mirroring the unusually young age of offenders in Stockport. In contrast, there were fewer younger victims in Lancashire (25%) and Bristol (23%). (Relatively small numbers should be borne in mind.)[42]

In all BCUs except Bristol, victims of phone robbery were younger than victims of other types of robbery (Figure 7.2).[43]

Figure 7.2 Percentage of victims under 18: phone and non-phone robbery (BCU information)

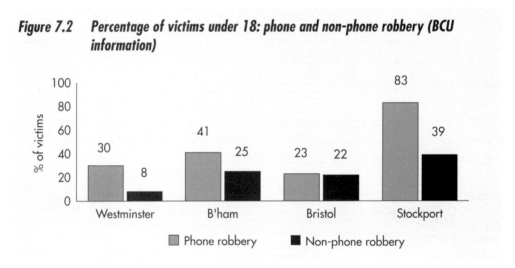

The age profile of victims and suspects (phone robberies)

Figure 7.3 compares the age profiles of victims and suspects for the BCUs. They do not match particularly well. The age of victims was more evenly distributed.[44] For instance, over half of offenders were aged 15, 16 or 17, but only a quarter of victims were. There were thus more older victims than older suspects.[45] There were also more younger victims than younger suspects, although the point made earlier about suspects perhaps being judged to be older than they really are need to be borne in mind here. On the face of it, then, this suggests offenders prey on victims both younger and older than themselves.

---

42 Table A7.2 in Appendix A has details for the forces, and Table A7.3 for the BCUs.
43 Overall, only 29% of phone robbery victims were aged 25 or over as against 54% of non-phone victims.
44 For instance, while the peak age of victims (15) was fairly similar to that of suspects (17), 15 year-old victims were only 8 per cent of all victims, whereas the 17 year-old suspects were 19% of all suspects.
45 Over 18 year olds constituted 61% of all victims compared with 44% for suspects. Less than 1 per cent of suspects were aged 35 or over as against 11% of victims.

Figure 7.3   The age profile of victims and suspects (BCU information)

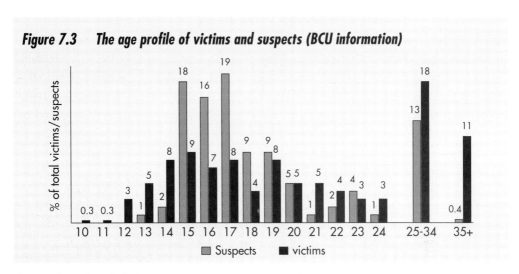

Age and gender of victims

It was possible to examine the age and gender of victims together in three forces.[46] Female victims were older than males in all three forces. Figure 7.4 gives the average picture[47] . The pattern was very similar in the four BCUs. Three-quarters of female victims were aged 18 or over compared with just over half (57%) of male victims.

Figure 7.4   Age of victims by gender (MPD, West Midlands and Avon and Somerset average)

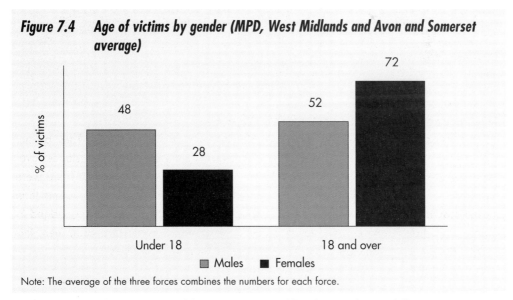

Note: The average of the three forces combines the numbers for each force.

Female victims of non-phone robbery were also older than males. A full 92% were 18 or more, compared to 72% of males.

46 Staffordshire, Lancashire and Merseyside did not give figures for age by gender while GMP used different age bands.
47 Further details are in Table A7.2 in Appendix A.

Age in relation to different types of mobile phone robbery (BCU information)

In Stockport and Westminster, there was little difference in the age profile of victims who had only a phone taken, and those who had a phone stolen along with other things. In Bristol and Birmingham, though, victims of phone-only robberies were younger than others.[48] It is difficult to say whether young victims are specifically targeted for a phone, or whether this is the most valuable item they have to offer.

Trends in the age of victims

Looking at phone robberies between 1998/99 and 2000/01 in the GMP suggests that the proportion of younger victims has increased. In 1998/99 and 1999/00, 35% of victims were under 19, but in 2000–01 46% were.[49] We cannot say from this whether younger children are being targeted more, since the GMP gave no details about any change in the age profile of victims of non-phone robberies. It might be that younger children feature more in phone robberies simply as a consequence of the greater likelihood of them owning a phone, and the fact that they are probably especially likely to report the loss of a phone to the police (as it will be an important item to them).

Ethnicity of victims

White victims were the vast majority in each of the six police forces providing information (Figure 7.5). Asians were next most often targeted in phone robberies. This was particularly so in the West Midlands (where they constituted nearly a quarter of victims) and in the MPD. (In both areas, the resident Asian population is somewhat larger than elsewhere, but still well below the victim proportion.) A relatively small proportion of victims were black. The highest figure was in the MPD (11% of victims).

Figure 7.5   Ethnicity of victims, by police force

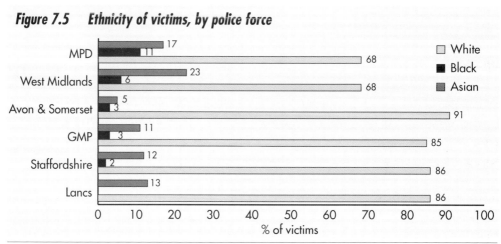

According to the BCU information, white victims were particularly dominant in Stockport and Bristol (Table 7.4). In Stockport, as seen, white *offenders* operated most often, so white-on-white incidents were most common. In Bristol, though, black offenders were more common than whites, so this suggests a different pattern.

Table 7.4 **Ethnicity of victims in each BCU**

	White %	Black %	Asian %	Other %	Total victims
Westminster	65	13	13	10	96
Birmingham	79	20	1	-	87
Bristol	92	3	5	-	123
Stockport	98	-	2	-	63

Asians were the least likely victims in Birmingham in direct contrast with the findings in the 'host' force, the West Midlands (see Figure 7.4 above). In Birmingham a fifth of victims were black (the highest proportion in any of the four BCUs), although in the West Midlands as a whole the proportion was smaller. While force level and BCU data showed general similarities with respect to the age of victim, then, ethnicity appears to be far more sensitive to the local area.

Trends in the ethnicity of victims

Data from GMP indicates that there has been a slight increase in the proportion of white victims between 1998/99, when they formed 79%, and 2000/01 (85%). There has been a corresponding decrease in Asian victims – from 15% to 11%.

Whether the phone was in use or on display

Information was collected from the BCUs' phone robberies as to whether phones were being used or were on display when incidents took place. In 23% of incidents overall this was the case, although the figure for Westminster was higher at 40%. As the visibility of a phone was only noted if case files mentioned it, the figures could be higher.

It is difficult to align the BCU information with that from the On Track survey (Section 2) since this covered all incidents, not just robberies. Nonetheless, the two sets of figures suggest that a fair proportion of victims are targeted when it is evident they have a phone.

Offenders more often, though, take a phone when it would not be immediately evident that the victim had one.

The time of offences

The BCU records also provided some information on the time that offences occurred. Figure 7.6 shows the picture for phone and non-phone robberies. In fact, there was relatively little difference. Very slightly more phone robberies took place in the afternoon, but the larger difference was in the small hours of the night when there was a bigger proportion of phone robberies

This information spanned January to March 2001, weighted most heavily to January. Lighter and warmer evenings at other times of the year might increase the proportion of evening and night robberies.

Figure 7.6   Time of occurrence: phone and non-phone robberies (BCU information)

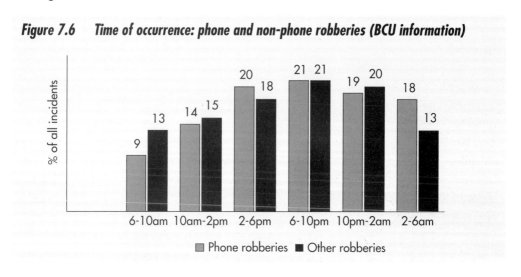

The indications are that these early hours phone robberies mainly involved victims over 18. Robberies against those over 18 peaked during the early hours as well as late night (Figure 7.7). In contrast, nearly six in ten phone robberies against those under 18 took place between 2pm and 10pm. Different activity patterns will underlie the difference to an extent.

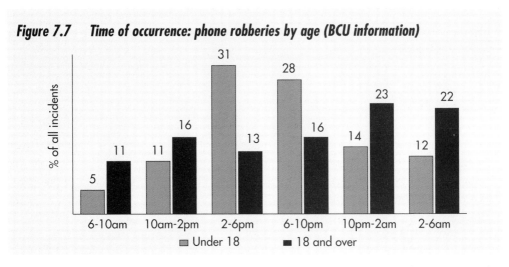

Figure 7.7   Time of occurrence: phone robberies by age (BCU information)

The picture for non-phone robberies was very similar. This, then, provides no particular support for the idea that 'after-school' incidents are special to phone robberies.

The day of the week

The overall picture from the BCUs was that phone robberies were not that unevenly spread across the week, although there was a peak on Saturday (Figure 7.8). The picture varied somewhat by BCU, though relatively small numbers preclude firm conclusions. There was even less difference across the week for non-phone robberies, though the Saturday peak was still evident.

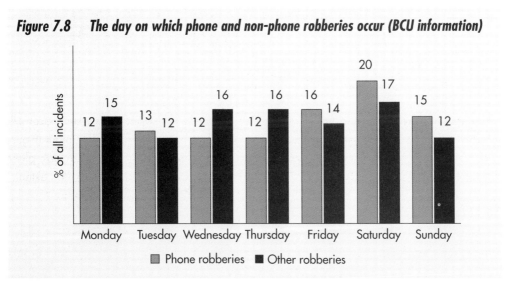

Figure 7.8   The day on which phone and non-phone robberies occur (BCU information)

8   Conclusions

This report has presented unique results on thefts involving mobile phones in England and Wales. The work done has not explored different types of mobile phone crime: for instance, subscription fraud, or the problem of warehouse theft relative to street crime. Rather, it has concentrated mainly on presenting figures on the overall extent of phone theft, and how this has changed recently. Police information and results from sample surveys are used in the main. Particular attention has been paid to the question of how far recent robbery figures have been fuelled by phone theft.

The main findings are discussed in the summary, and those particularly relevant to prevention are taken up later. But other some key points are:

- According to a MORI survey, 5 per cent of 11-16 year olds had a phone stolen last year. The less representative On Track survey put the figure higher still. This level of risk is well in excess of that for adults. The survey indications, too, are that the risks of having a phone stolen in a robbery or theft from the person are much higher for youngsters than adults.

- There were an estimated 330,000 offences involving phones recorded by the police in England and Wales in 2000-01 (6 per cent of all recorded crime). This will underestimate the total, as not all thefts will be reported. Some reports may be false allegations – although we did not judge the number to be large.

- About 20-25% of all thefts take place in the course of robbery and thefts from the person (when phones are on or near their owner, but no force or threat of force is used). The proportion for teenagers appears higher.

- Estimates indicate that over a quarter (28%) of robberies involved a phone in 2000/01, up from 8% two years ago. (In the MPD a full 36% of robberies involved phones.) Even more thefts from the person involved a phone (a third). These are much higher figures than evidenced by the BCS – perhaps because it excludes young victims, and thefts involving a phone are more often reported to the police.

- Phone robbers appear younger than other robbers: a third of those accused were aged 15 or 16, but there were differences across area, illustrating diverse patterns.

- About two-thirds of offenders were black in three out of seven areas. The proportion was about half in two of the other four areas.

- More than two-thirds of phone robberies involve offenders working with others. The figure was 80% for suspects under 18.

- Nearly half of all victims were under 18, with the peak at age 15 and 16. Victims of phone robbery were younger than victims of other types of robbery.

- Discussed in some detail was the rise in phone thefts. Figures from six forces show the number of recorded phone thefts has at least doubled between 1998/999 and 2000/01. There was a three-fold increase in two forces. BCS figures, though, show the increase in phone thefts since 1995 is much lower than the increase in subscribers.

- Particular attention was paid to how far the rise in 'acquisitive street crime' in England and Wales has been fuelled by phone theft. Some main pointers were:

  - The bigger increase in phone robberies and thefts from the person than in other offences involving phones.

  - The higher increase in phone robberies over the last three years that involve only a phone, as opposed to a phone and other items.

  - Evidence from Manchester that the proportion of younger victims has increased somewhat between 1998/99 and 200/01.

At the end of the day, though, it is difficult to say for certain whether phones are to blame *per se*. Increasing ownership clearly means that phones have become an obvious 'stealable' item and their theft in greater numbers may simply be because there are more around. More false allegations as a corollary of higher ownership may also be implicated in the rising figures. In addition, there may be more reporting to the police as phone ownership has grown in particular among youngsters for whom a phone will be a particularly valuable item.

Some technical points

It may not be clear to everyone how phones can be used after they are stolen, and what technical blocks can be put in place. It is useful, then, to outline some technical points.

Mobile phones consist of two separate elements: the handset and the SIM card. An IMEI (International Mobile Equipment Identity) number identifies the handset.[50] The mobile (MSISDN) number identifies the SIM card.

There are already some basic security measures available to protect existing phones. SIM cards have password or Personal Identification Number (PIN) protection mechanisms built into them to prevent unauthorised use. However, the PIN is of limited use when a phone is switched on when stolen. It will remain active till the batteries run down, and even then these can be recharged while the phone is still working. Phone users seem reluctant to use PIN numbers although obviously they provide some safeguard against unauthorised use of the SIM.

All operators are able to disable the SIM number. However, since this does not block the handset itself, one strategy for thieves is simply to insert a new SIM card. They can be easily and legitimately obtained for about £20, and the Feltham offenders spoke of "dodgy" markets where they could be picked up for £5 or less.

Three operators can disable the handset if users know their IMEI number. A particular problem is that few users in the UK seem to know their IMEI number, perhaps not appreciating its significance in dealing with theft. Another problem is that a handset barred on one network can be used on another UK network (or one abroad) with a valid SIM card for that network.[51]

Even operators who can block handsets face the problem that they can be unblocked by changing the IMEI number (sometimes known as 'tumbling' or 're-chipping'). This requires specialised equipment but this is commercially available for valid users, and at a lower price (c. £30) on the black market.

---

50 It is a fifteen-digit serial number.
51 A further problem is that IMEI numbers are not unique (about 10% are not) and so barring them can affect legitimate users.

Why phones are stolen

Phones will be stolen and used as criminal currency for a variety of reasons. Some phones will be stolen simply because they are part of the general 'pickings' of people's current possessions. Others will be more specifically targeted, no doubt. In either event, phones are attractive as small, fairly valuable items for which ready re-sale markets exist among those without a phone, or with an old model. One market will be dubious outlets at which phones can be reprogrammed and possibly sent abroad to countries with growing demand. The opportunities here get attention from the police and from operators (who lose money from the use of airtime). But hard information is difficult to pin down.

The plethora of phones around – left for instance casually on counter tops in bars, or on the shelf near the front door at home – also makes them relatively accessible to thieves. In the case of street crime, too, potential thieves can easily spot someone with a phone. It is difficult to say how much truth there is in the contention of offenders in Feltham Young Offenders' Institution that owners' ostentatious use of phones causes a degree of irritation that provokes theft – but it might give users pause for thought. Aside from ostentatious use, the fact that nearly a quarter of phone robberies according to the BCU data involved phones that were being used or on display testifies to phone visibility being a factor in theft.[52]

There is also the simple technological fascination of mobile phones and the way in which they expand social interaction. For the Feltham boys, they were an indispensable social crutch. Their loss of phones in custody was said to be one of the worst elements of the deprivation of their liberty.

Finally, a notion that has currency among some police officers is that phones are stolen in the process of 'taxing'. Here, the phone theft *per se* is less important than groups of offenders exerting control, establishing territorial rights, and showing 'who's who' by penalising street users (in particular young ones) through phone theft amongst things. We know of no hard evidence, though, as to the scale of this problem.

The uses to which stolen phones are put

The research only addressed this through the Feltham boys who gave some clues. The phones themselves seemed the attractive commodity. Less so were the free calls available

---

52 A robbery analyst in Merseyside suggests the current fashion for text messaging (with many operators now providing free messaging facilities to encourage use) means that messaging owners are vulnerable because they are insufficiently alert to their surroundings.

until an owner with a contract phone got the number blocked, or the Pay As You Go (PAYG) card ran out (which might be quite soon as the vast majority of cards sold are for £10). Certainly, advantage was taken of the free calls, and if the model was a "tatty" one, the phone might simply then be thrown away (though the batteries sometimes kept).

But more important was the apparently ready market for phones. The Feltham boys were not in much accord about the price that stolen phones could be sold for – perhaps because they had different market opportunities. Some mentioned figures of £10-£20; others said a good phone could fetch up to £60. The fact that new SIM cards can be got easily and cheaply was also important for those wanting to keep or pass on a "flashy" phone. There was also mention of 'everlasting top-up' cards on sale for £150, one said.[53]

A focus group held with nine sixth-formers in Pimlico School in London early in 2001 also said local knowledge was that phones were stolen mainly for the value of the handset. The group also testified to the ready market for good phones at cheap prices such that there was little need for offenders to turn to 'dealers'. All the pupils had been offered stolen phones, and without revealing what had happened, were prepared to admit that they were tempted if the price was right.

A pointer to the uses of stolen phones as well as the reasons for theft comes from a tracking exercise of 100 stolen phones organised by the MPD and BT Cellnet, with the co-operation of other operators. The purpose was to see if stolen phones reappeared on one or other UK network. The results showed that about 25% did so. The remainder either could have been reprogrammed with a different IMEI number for use in the UK or abroad, or they could have simply been discarded. To the extent they were discarded, this might confirm the 'taxing' notion. But equally, it could mean that some phones are simply not felt worth bothering with.

Prevention: some issues

There is no attempt here to fully address the range of preventive options. Rather, brief mention is made first of a few issues to do with (i) technical solutions, (ii) property marking and (iii) 'bombing'. Attention is then paid to the specific preventive implications of the present results.

---

53 Other uses mentioned were to change phones with bad reception, and to get a new number to fend off an unwanted girlfriend.

Technical solutions

The issues to do with possible technical solutions to phone theft are complicated, and the networks appear cautious about revealing what they can or are willing to do given commercial interests. Suffice it to make three points though:

- The most obvious solution seems to be disabling the handset - since if it cannot be used when a phone is reported lost or stolen, the point of stealing it would go. This was fully obvious to the Feltham boys. However, a cross-industry group has failed to come up with any solution that would cost a price they would be prepared to pay.

- Technical solutions, then, would need to be reasonably cheap. This is because the financial impact of 'commonplace' theft for the phone industry is probably small, and may be more than compensated for by victims simply buying another phone. (Larger-scale organised crime involving 're-chipping' of phone, warehouse theft, and selling phones abroad may be another matter for the industry.) Technological curbs that cost the industry more than they stand to lose will clearly be resisted, notwithstanding central government pressure. At the moment the operators claim that measures to disable handsets would be too expensive to consider, especially given ageing technology that will be replaced by 3G devices. Phone cloning of analogue phones in the United States in the earlier 1990s posed a different scenario. Here, a cloned phone could build up losses for operators of several thousand dollars (Clarke *et al.*, 2001; DTI, 2000). Aided by the advent of digital technology, the operators found a solution.

- Solutions also need to be practical so that phone users are not discouraged by complex registration or usage procedures when setting up new accounts or changing phones.

Property marking

Property marking has a long tradition in crime prevention and evidence of its success in some arenas (Laycock, 1997) has made it an obvious contender in relation to mobile phones.[54] A positive, if small, effect has been claimed for an initiative in Waltham Forest with respect to street crime against school children, although no data is given.[55] The interchangeable elements of phones (covers for instance) pose some limitations. The style conscious might also baulk at defacing their phones with something as 'naff' as their name

---

54 Schemes have been started, for instance, in Newham, Waltham Forest, Greenwich, Barnet and Lewisham.
55 MPD paper on street crime by PRS (5).

and address. Nonetheless, promoting some irremovable form of identification on a phone is a sensible idea.

The IMEI number on mobile phones is of course already a technical version of property marking. Although there are some limits to how far blocking these would curtail all criminal opportunities, owners should pay more attention to keeping a record of their IMEI number. A recent Home Office leaflet on preventing phone theft has stressed the need for this.

'Bombing'

The Dutch police in Amsterdam have claimed great success for an operation in which the police 'bomb' phone numbers belonging to phones reported as stolen with a continuous stream of messages that effectively preclude normal phone use. There were indications of an initial fall in street phone robberies, which may have been more the result of a substantial publicity campaign than 'bombing' itself, which in reality involved fairly few phones. The most recent figures are less favourable, no doubt due to the fact that offenders have realised the chance of being 'bombed' are small. Less resource intensive automated 'bombing' procedures might increase the risks for offenders, but this would incur additional costs. The tracking of handsets through IMEI numbers would also require the co-operation of all operators.

For what it is worth, the Feltham boys' reaction to a description of 'bombing' was bemusement. In their view, avoiding it would be simply a matter of stealing another phone on the expectation that its loss would not be reported, or that the police would not be able to keep up.

The results of the MPD/Cellnet exercise which showed that about one in four tracked stolen phones were subsequently used on a network perhaps also questions 'bombing' initiatives, since few stolen phones might be caught by them.

Prevention: the present results

There are a number of pointers from the present results. Some general ones are discussed first, then those to do with street crime.

The main areas of risk

The BCS results indicate that adults are as likely to fall victim when a phone is left in a car, when their house is broken into, or when they leave the phone unattended somewhere else. The chances of phones being stolen in either a robbery or a theft from the person are no higher. The lesson from this is that phone owners need to be alerted not just to the risks of thefts in street crime.

The risks for teenagers

There are no firm estimates for teenagers of the *relative* risks of phones being stolen in robbery, thefts from the person, or when the phone has been left unattended. The indication from the On Track survey, though, is that the gap between adults and teenagers in risks of phone 'contact crime' is particularly wide – greater than the perhaps five-fold difference in overall risks.

The higher risks may be because teenagers are less careful with their phones, or more likely to be out and about in vulnerable places. In any event, initiatives targeted at teenagers, including school programmes, are fully justified. Despite some limitations mentioned earlier of PIN numbers to lock the phone, using them is a simple measure to promote. If their use got to a critically high level, the immediate reward for thieves of making free calls might cease. It may be that some offenders would escalate tactics to get the owner to reveal the PIN or password, but it would very pessimistic to assume that all would do so.

Another simple message is for particular care to be taken after the Christmas period when many new phones are bought or older models exchanged for better ones. Both figures from the MPD and New South Wales show increases in phone theft in January.

Has phone theft peaked?

The results from police forces indicate that the rise in both all phone thefts and phone robberies was greater between 1998/999 and 1999/00 than between 1999/00 and 2000/01. All phone thefts increased by an estimated 65% between 1998/99 and the next year, but by a lower 41% between that one and 2000/01. The respective figures for phone robberies were 144% and 96%. The BCS do not show quite the same picture, although its trend estimates are somewhat fragile.

The question then is whether the tide is turning. Phones are perhaps less of a 'must have' item, simply because they are now commonplace. It could also conceivably be that owners, alerted to the risks, are taking greater care. On the other hand, new models come rapidly onto the market and the young in particular have great appetite for them. Any new 'generation' of phones offering substantially enhanced facilities could well generate a new 'crime harvest' - as was the case when better models of car stereo equipment came onto the market (Light and Nee, 1993). Perhaps the main moral to date is that phone manufacturers and others should have thought in advance about the criminogenic potential of phones. Hindsight then tells us that better security needs to be a key issue for the next generation of phones.

The implications of the current results for street phone crime

Although the current work focused specifically on robbery, there is good reason to think that many of its pointers will apply equally to theft from the person involving phones. Taken together, they can be conveniently labelled street phone crime. A number of results are worth highlighting from a preventive point of view.

- Phone robberies are predominantly a male-on-male event: 77% of all incidents in the four city centre areas were. Young male phone users, then, have cause to be the most wary. Probably, though, women and girls are more vulnerable to theft from the person, which often involve thefts from bags. Risks of unattended phones are likely to be fairly equal.

- A third of incidents against women involved female offenders or mixed groups although this was rare when men were targeted. Women, then, have cause to be more wary than men about groups in which girls or women act suspiciously. They still, though, should be more wary about men.

- Female victims have a broader age spread than male victims. Whether this is because offenders think adult men might put up more resistance is difficult to say. In any event, though, women across the age spectrum need to be cautious.

- Street phone crime is more common in city centre areas. This may be because the types of offenders in the business of stealing phones may frequent city centres themselves more. Or busy central areas may provide the easiest pickings from other young socialites or busy shoppers. In any event, the risks in city centres are worth emphasising.

- In city centres nearly a quarter of robberies took place when the phone was being used or on show, and this may be an underestimate. This points to the need for more judicious use of phones in public places. Whether users will trade phone companionship for safety remains to be seen.

- Street users should be aware that younger people are most likely to be potential phone thieves in many areas. A third of accused offenders were aged 15 or 16, and the proportion under 18 in the city areas was higher than for other robberies.

- Youngsters acting in groups are likely to be involved: over two-thirds of offenders in city centres operated with others, and a full 80% of suspects were under 18.

- There are no strong lessons as to when people should be most on guard. Those under 18 faced higher risks in the afternoon and evening, but this is when they are likely to be out most. Those over 18 were most at risk late at night and in the early hours.

References

Briscoe, S. (2001) *The problem of mobile phone theft.* Crime and Justice Bulletin No. 56. Sydney: New South Wales Bureau of Crime Statistics and Research.

Clarke, R.V.G (1997). 'Deterring obscene phone calls: the New Jersey experience'. In Clarke, R.V.G, *Situational Crime Prevention: successful case studies* (2nd edition). New York: Harrow and Heston.

Clarke, R., Kemper, R. and Wyckoff, L. (2001) 'Controlling cell phone fraud in the US: lessons for the UK 'Foresight' Prevention Initiative.' *Security Journal* 14, pp.7-22.

Department of Trade and Industry (2000) *Turning the Corner.* Report of Foresight Programme's Crime Prevention Panel. London: Department of Trade and Industry.

East, K. and Campbell, S. (2001) Aspects of Crime: Young Offenders 1999. (Internet only). http://www.homeoffice.gov.uk/rds/adhocpubs1.html

Flood-Page, C., Campbell, S. Harrington, V. and Miller, J. (2000).Youth Crime: Findings from the 1998/99 Youth Lifestyles Survey. Home Office Research Study No.209. Home Office: London.

Grabosky, P.N. and Smith, R.G. (1998) *Crime in the Digital Age.* The Federation Press: New South Wales.

Home Office (2000) Section 95: Statistics on Race and the Criminal Justice System. A Home Office publication under section 95 of the Criminal Justice Act 1991.

Kershaw, C., Chivette-Matthews, N. Thomas, C. and Aust, R.. (2001) *The 2001 British Crime Survey.* Home Office Statistical Bulletin 18/0. London: Home Office.

Laycock, G. (1997). 'Operation identification or the power of publicity. ' In Clarke, R.V.G, *Situational Crime Prevention: successful case studies* (2nd edition). New York: Harrow and Heston.

Lewis, D. and Mhalnga, B. (2001) 'A life of crime: the hidden truth behind criminal activity.' *The Journal of the Market Research Society, International Journal of Market Research*, Vol.40, pp.217-240.

Light, R. and Nee, C. (1993). *Car Theft: the offenders' perspective*. Home Office Research Study No. 130. London: Home Office.

MORI (2001) *Youth Survey 2001*. Research Study conducted for the Youth Justice Board.

Parliamentary Office of Science and Technology. (1995). 'Mobile phone theft'. *Science in Parliament, Vol. 52, No. 6*, pp 27-30.

Povey, D. and colleagues (2001) *Recorded crime, England and Wales*. Home Office Statistical Bulletin 12/01. London: Home Office.

Pease, K. (1997) 'Predicting the Future: the Roles of Routine Activity and Rational Choice Theory' in Newman, G., Clarke, R and Shoham, S.G. (eds.) *Rational Choice and Situational Crime Prevention: Theoretical Foundations*. Aldershot: Dartmouth.

Appendix A

Additional tables

Table A2.1 *Proportion of each offence type involving a phone theft in 2000/01: four police forces*

	Metropolitan Police District	West Midlands	Avon & Somerset	Greater Manchester Police
	%	%	%	%
Personal robbery	39	27	22	20
Theft from the person	35	36	32	33
Other theft	16	8	10	6
Theft from vehicle	15	10	8	9
Burglary (dwelling)	14	9	7	11
Burglary (non dwelling)	12	3	2	8
Commercial robbery	<1	6	0	0

Note: The figure for GMP combines personal and commercial robbery within the 'personal robbery' category. All figures include attempts.

Table A4.1 *Percentage change in thefts involving phones in six forces*

	1998/98 to 1998/99	1998/99 to 1999/2000	1999/2000 to 2000/01
Kent	46	55	50
MPD	na	56	37
West Midlands	na	110	45
Avon & Somerset	na	65	44
GMP	na	64	55
Lancashire	na	84	74

na: data not available

Table A4.2   The proportion of thefts from the person involving phones over the last three years, six forces

	1998/98	1999/2000	2000/01
MPD	18	24	35
West Midlands	14	24	36
Avon & Somerset	13	22	32
GMP	11	21	35
Lancashire	6	11	28
Kent	8	16	25
Average	15	21	33

Note: The average takes account of the share of thefts from the person in metropolitan and non-metropolitan areas in the sampled forces.

Table A5.1   Robbery and phone robbery trends

	All robberies N	Robberies involving phones N	% of all robberies involving phones	% increase in phone robberies	% increase for all robberies	% increase in robbery excluding those involving phones
MPD						
98/99	26,300	3,220	12			
99/00	36,300	7,610	21	136	38	24
00/01	41,000	14,860	36	95	13	-9
West Midlands						
98/99	7,300	510	7			
99/00	10,100	1,520	15	196	38	20
00/01	11,400	2,750	24	81	12	0
Avon and Somerset						
98/99	1,800	80	4			
99/00	2,400	260	11	225	30	21
00/01	2,800	560	20	112	16	4
GMP						
98/99	7,600	410	5			
99/00	8,600	950	11	130	13	6
00/01	9,900	1,980	20	109	15	3
Lancashire						
98/99	1,000	30	3			
99/00	1,100	90	10	242	8	1
00/01	1,200	150	13	73	16	10
Kent						
98/99	700	20	3			
99/00	800	40	5	95	16	14
00/01	1,000	130	13	222	21	10
Average		*Estimated*				
98/99	66,800	5,510	8			
99/00	84,300	13,410	16	144	26	16
00/01	95,200	26,290	28	96	13	-3

Notes: The figures for all robberies are those published, but rounded. Some differ slightly from the totals provided by forces. The figures for robberies involving phones are unrounded. Percentage increases are based on unrounded numbers

Kent figures exclude property classified as mobile phone accessories.

The average takes account of the share of robbery in the sampled metropolitan and non-metropolitan forces relative to metropolitan and non-metropolitan forces as a whole. The average is weighted within the two sectors.

Table A5.2 *Personal robberies for phone-only incidents and those in which phones were taken with other items*

	1998/999		1999/00		2000/01	
	Total phone robberies	% involving theft of a phone *only*	Total phone robberies	% involving theft of a phone *only*	Total phone robberies	% involving theft of a phone *only*
	N		N		N	
Avon & Somerset	78	38	258	31	557	39
West Midlands	500	28	1475	30	2659	36
GMP	412	26	946	29	1975	36

Note: Figures for Avon and Somerset and the West Midlands are for personal robbery. Figures for GMP are for total robbery (personal and commercial).

Table A6.1 *Age of accused: percentage of all those accused (police force information)*

	10-13 %	14-17 %	18-20 %	21-34 %	35+ %	Total	Total N
Metropolitan Police District							
Males	6	59	19	14	3	100%	1783
Females	15	66	5	9	4	100%	237
West Midlands 00/01							
Males	5	45	21	24	6	100%	646
Females	3	69	12	16	1	100%	77
Avon and Somerset							
Males	3	38	20	35	3	100%	60

Table A6.2   Age of suspects: percentage of all suspects (BCU information)

	0-9 %	10-13 %	14-17 %	All under 18 %	18-20 %	21-34 %	35+ %	Total	Total N
Westminster									
All	-	1	57	58	21	20	1	100%	217
Males	-	1	59	59	20	21	1	100%	198
Females	-	-	42	42	37	16	5	100%	19
Birmingham									
All	1	1	53	55	16	28	-	100%	183
Males	1	1	52	54	16	31	-	100%	170
Females	8	-	69	77	23	-	-	100%	13
Bristol									
All	-	1	27	28	26	44	1	100%	144
Males	-	1	26	27	27	44	1	100%	140
Females	-	-	50	50	-	50	-	100%	4
Stockport									
All	-	1	70	71	26	3	-	100%	225
Males	-	1	69	70	26	3	-	100%	206
Females	-	-	74	74	26	-	-	100%	19

Note: Where the age of a suspect was given as a band the mid-point has been used for the purposes of analysis. Because of the small number of female suspects, the figures should be treated with caution.

Table A6.3   Ethnicity of suspects (BCU information)

	White %	Black %	Asian %	Other %	Total N All suspects = 100%
Westminster					
All	29	65	1	5	219
Males	31	63	2	5	200
Females	16	70	0	3	19
Birmingham					
All	9	54	34	4	186
Males	9	53	35	3	176
Females	8	68	16	8	10
Bristol					
All	31	63	3	3	168
Males	30	64	3	3	164
Females	100	-	-	-	4
Stockport					
All	76	10	3	11	209
Males	77	10	3	10	193
Females	69	6	6	19	16

Table A6.4   Number of suspects for each offence

	Male suspects %	Female suspects %
Lone suspect	31	26
Two suspects	33	39
3-9 suspects	32	35
10-20 suspects	4	-
	100%	100%
Total number of incidents	*293*	*23*

Note: The small number of female suspects means that these results should be treated with caution.

Table A6.5   Lone and multiple offenders (BCU information)

	Under 18 %	18 and over %
Lone offender	20	38
2 or more offenders	80	62
	100%	100%
Total number of incidents	*126*	*173*

Table A7.1   Breakdown of victims and offenders (percentages): phone and non-phone robberies (BCU information)

	Offenders			
	Male	Female	Mixed	N
Phone robberies				
Victims				
Male	*77*	*1*	*2*	*278*
Female	*14*	*4*	*2*	*69*
All incidents	*313*	*18*	*16*	*100%*
Non-phone robberies				
Victims				
Male	*71*	*1*	*4*	*409*
Female	*22*	*2*	*1*	*133*
All incidents	*503*	*16*	*23*	*100%*

Table A7.2 Age of victims, by gender (police force information)

	Up to 13 %	14-17 %	Under 18 %	18-20 %	21-34 %	35+ %	Total N
MPD							
All	9	34	**43**	14	31	12	*14685*
Males	9	39	**49**	15	26	10	*10834*
Females	8	20	**29**	10	44	17	*3851*
West Midlands 00/01							
All	5	35	**40**	18	29	13	*2847*
Males	5	38	**44**	19	28	10	*2264*
Females	4	22	**27**	15	35	24	*583*
Avon and Somerset							
All	6	30	**37**	20	30	13	*550*
Males	6	33	**39**	21	32	9	*423*
Females	7	22	**29**	17	26	28	*127*
Staffordshire							
All	12	42	**54**	18	18	10	*50*
Lancashire							
All	4	21	**25**	20	34	21	*154*

Notes: Males and females may underestimate the 'all' figure as for some cases gender was not stated. Staffordshire and Lancashire's figures for age were not given by gender. GMP used different age bands.

Table A7.3 Age of victims (BCU information)

	Up to 13 %	14-17 %	Under 18 %	18-20 %	21-34 %	35+ %	**Total**	**Total victims**
Westminster	7	23	**30**	16	45	9	*100%*	*97*
Birmingham	13	28	**41**	19	26	15	*100%*	*86*
Bristol	3	20	**23**	23	40	15	*100%*	*120*
Stockport	16	67	**82**	3	13	2	*100%*	*64*

Note: There were too female victims in each BCU to analyse separately: Stockport n= 8, Bristol n=29, Birmingham n=12 and Westminster= 22.

Table A7.4   Age and types of robbery (BCU information)

	0-9 %	10-13 %	14-17 %	18-20 %	21-34 %	35+ %	Total victims
Bristol							
Mobile and additional items stolen	0	2	14	19	46	19	88
Only a mobile stolen	0	3	38	31	25	3	32
Birmingham							
Mobile and additional items stolen	0	13	25	18	27	18	56
Only a mobile stolen	0	13	33	20	23	10	30
Westminster							
Mobile and additional items stolen	0	7	24	16	45	9	58
Only a mobile stolen	0	8	21	15	46	10	39
Stockport							
Mobile and additional items stolen	0	17	66	5	12	-	41
Only a mobile stolen	0	13	70	-	13	4	23

Note: Robberies where a mobile was asked for but not stolen (attempts) are not included.

RDS Publications

Requests for Publications

Copies of our publications and a list of those currently available may be obtained from:

Home Office
Research, Development and Statistics Directorate
Communication Development Unit
Room 275, Home Office
50 Queen Anne's Gate
London SW1H 9AT
Telephone: 020 7273 2084 (answerphone outside of office hours)
Facsimile: 020 7222 0211
E-mail: publications.rds@homeoffice.gsi.gov.uk

alternatively

why not visit the RDS web-site at
          Internet: http://www.homeoffice.gov.uk/rds/index.htm

where many of our publications are available to be read on screen or downloaded for printing.